PRAISE FOR *THE SMALL-TOWN PAGAN'S*
SURVIVAL GUIDE

"Bronwen's style conveys the information clearly and succinctly. The book is worthwhile and fun. We freely recommend it to anyone in a town of any size!"

—Elspeth and Nybor, cofounders of the
spiritual path The Haven Way

"I found this book to be a wonderful, friendly open door for those who live removed from the Pagan amenities and social contact that city witches take for granted. Living in a small town can leave one feeling lonely and isolated, but Bronwen's warm and friendly book, filled with ideas and comments from many, will always assure you that you are not alone. You city folk will find a great deal of wisdom as well!"

—Rev. Paul Beyerl, author of
The Master Book of Herbalism

"Incredibly informative, well-written, and lighthearted. This book gives hope to all the Pagans making their way in our various hinterlands, whether solitary or weathering the social storms in tiny groups."

—Raven Kaldera, author of *The Urban Primitive*

D0092791

——— THE ———
SMALL-TOWN PAGAN'S
Survival Guide

© JIM HOGG PHOTOGRAPHY

About the Author

Bronwen Forbes has lived in both big cities and small towns and has experienced the advantages and drawbacks of both. She co-founded Free Spirit Alliance and has taught at various Pagan festivals, Pride Days, and conferences across North America. She is also the author of *Make Merry in Step and Song: A Seasonal Treasury of Music, Mummer's Plays & Celebrations in the English Folk Tradition.*

BRONWEN FORBES

————— THE —————

SMALL-TOWN PAGAN'S
Survival Guide

HOW TO THRIVE
IN ANY COMMUNITY

Llewellyn Publications
Woodbury, Minnesota

FIRST EDITION
First Printing, 2011

Cover art © Paul Oglesby / AA Reps, Inc.
Cover design by Lisa Novak
Editing by Brett Fechheimer
Interior photograph © Sylvia Forbes

Llewellyn Publications is a registered trademark of Llewellyn Worldwide Ltd.

Library of Congress Cataloging-in-Publication Data

Forbes, Bronwen, 1963–
  The small-town pagan's survival guide : how to thrive in any community /
  Bronwen Forbes. — 1st ed.
      p.   cm.
  Includes bibliographical references and index.
  ISBN 978-0-7387-2622-9
  1. Neopagans—United States. 2. Small cities—United States.
  3. Religious life—Neopaganism. 4. Cities and towns—Religious
aspects—Neopaganism. I. Title.
  BP605.N46F67 2011
  299'.940973—dc22

                        2010049168

Llewellyn Publications
A Division of Llewellyn Worldwide Ltd.
2143 Wooddale Drive
Woodbury, MN 55125-2989
www.llewellyn.com

Printed in the United States of America

Other Books by This Author

*Make Merry in Step and Song: A Seasonal Treasury of Music,
Mummer's Plays & Celebrations in the English Folk Tradition*

For

Ravenna, Spiritrunner, K, Noey, Julia, Donna Hames, Becca, Jenn, Evy, Witch of the Woods, Kathleen from North Dakota, Deanna Eberlin, Moondancer, Keltasia, Cordelia, Lisa McSherry, Ruth Merriam, Rowen Brianna, Fergus, Kim Schaufenbuel, Andrea Covey, Darren, and Iris.

You have taught me so much.

Acknowledgments

It is always true that one person does not write a book in a vacuum. In this case, I have fifty survey respondents to thank, especially the twenty-three who have agreed to let themselves be quoted in this book either in their own words as they completed my survey or as interviewees on specific topics. They are as much co-authors as they are contributors; their wisdom and experiences have taught me a great deal.

My thanks also to Elysia Gallo of Llewellyn Worldwide for once again believing in me and what I have to say. She and production editor Brett Fechheimer are truly saints for not panicking when a family medical crisis delayed my work on the final manuscript.

I have tried to be as accurate as possible when recording the population of the towns the survey respondents live in, unless the respondents did not want their town specifically mentioned. For this I have used the numbers provided by the U.S. Census Bureau for its 2009 Population Estimates Program. I apologize for any inaccuracies.

I could not have written this book without the help and support of my husband, A. G., and my daughter Rose. Not only have their own experiences as small-town Pagans been chronicled here, but they've handled my telling of those experiences to perfect strangers with humor and grace. They were also the best traveling companions ever, for the now-famous "Walmart Altar Road Trip" recounted in chapter 4.

Finally, because of life and moving and finishing a bachelor's degree in journalism and a few other inexcusable excuses, there was a four-year gap between the time I originally sent out the survey to interested participants and when I actually started working on the book. During that time, several of my original respondents changed or dropped the e-mail addresses they used to send me their survey responses (the only way I had to reach them). Their comments have not been included in this book, since I had no way to get their signed permission to do so. One of those lost respondents didn't have a lot to say in her survey that was overly positive or negative, but the name she asked me to use if I quoted her told me everything I needed to know. She asked me to refer to her as "Silent."

On a very deep and personal level, this entire book is dedicated to all the "Silents" out there who were too frightened to say anything to me at all.

Bronwen Forbes

Baldwin City, Kansas

Summer 2010

Contents

Introduction

Some Basic Definitions

For the purposes of this book, if you think you are a Pagan, you are.

And if you think you live in a small town, you do.

After all, the definition of a twenty-first-century American Pagan is relative. Some use the term to define anything that isn't one of the "Big Three"—Christianity, Judaism, or Islam. Even within our own community, the term *Pagan* can encompass vastly different beliefs and practices, as illustrated by the following definition from the Pagan Pride Project:

> *A Pagan or Neo-Pagan is someone who self-identifies as a Pagan, and whose spiritual or religious*

> *practice or belief fits into one or more of the following*
> *categories:*
>
> • *Honoring, revering, or worshipping a Deity or Deities found*
>   *in pre-Christian, classical, aboriginal, or tribal mythology;*
>   *and/or*
>
> • *Practicing religion or spirituality based upon shamanism,*
>   *shamanic, or magickal practices; and/or*
>
> • *Creating new religion based on past Pagan religions and/or*
>   *futuristic views of society, community, and/or ecology;*
>
> • *Focusing religious or spiritual attention primarily on the Di-*
>   *vine Feminine. . . .*[1]

I can't tell you if you're Pagan or not. No one can. But if one of the definitions above closely describes what you do and think, or *want* to do or think (but may not know exactly how to yet), religiously speaking, then *I* think you're a Pagan.

The definition of "small town" is equally relative. If you grew up in New York City, then you probably think of Lubbock, Texas (population 225,859) as a small town. But if you grew up in Fayette, Ohio (population 1,281), then Lubbock is a big city to you. Likewise, I can't tell you if you live in a small town or not.

Let me give you an example: when I lived in the suburbs of Washington, DC, I knew I lived in a big city. Spiritually, my city offered three major Pagan festivals a year, a quarterly Pagan newspaper, four or five good occult shops, dozens of

---

1. "Who We Are," Pagan Pride Project, Inc. Online at http://www .paganpride.org/who/who.html.

botanicas (supply shops for those of the Santería, Voudon, and Yoruba faiths and a source of awesomely cheap glass-enclosed pillar candles), a monthly concert/lecture series, and more covens, classes, workshops, forums, and discussion groups in more traditions than one person could join in a lifetime. Washington, DC also offered me the opportunity to wear my pentacle and other Pagan jewelry as openly as I pleased twenty-four hours a day, seven days a week. Who cares about a little silver star-in-a-circle when the Hare Krishna standing behind me at Starbucks is wearing saffron robes, has a drum tucked under his arm, and sports a shaved head—except for one long ponytail?

In early 2000, for reasons I will discuss later in this book, I moved to Missouri and spent four years in a town of about 91,000 souls, a figure that included the student population of three colleges.

I was not prepared for a place where the nearest Pagan festival was three hours away and the local community only got together once a month for discussion and pizza. There were two covens—my husband and I started one of them—and a small student organization at one of the colleges. Oh, and the nearest Pagan shop was also about a three hours' drive away. I thought I had died and moved to hell.

Then, in 2004, my family and I moved *again* to a tiny town in rural New Mexico. The population, according to the sign at the town limits, was "twelve thousand friendly souls and a few old grouches." The nearest Pagan shop was now *four* to *five* hours away. There was no monthly community get-together at all. I had Pagan acquaintances who were afraid to be seen buying Harry Potter books, much less meeting openly in a restaurant or coffee shop to discuss (insert whispered tones here) *Paganism*. There were no concerts and the nearest coven was ninety miles away in Roswell (population 46,453).

There was, however, a very bad taste in the locals' minds about the word *Pagan* after some college students tried to start an on-campus study group only to be blasted in the town newspaper by every Baptist minister within a thirty-mile radius. And there are a lot of Baptist ministers in those parts. The Pagans weren't about to admit their religious affiliations after that, not even to their fellow practitioners, and the non-Pagans in the area eventually found something else to get all worked up about. But the college study group didn't last very long. Neither did my job, after the local university paper did the requisite "Let's interview a Witch for Halloween" article, with me as the interviewed Witch. But I will discuss all of this in detail later.

Comparatively speaking, that town in Missouri seemed like a spiritually rich place.

So my personal definition of "small town" has changed dramatically. And yours is probably different from mine.

The 2000 Census found that approximately 60 percent of all Americans live in (or in the suburbs of) a city with a minimum population of 200,000, which means that approximately 40 percent live in small towns and other rural areas. From this we can assume that approximately 40 percent of all Pagans live in (or in the suburbs of) a city with a population under 200,000.

Whether you've never met another Pagan in your life or have been part of a thriving community for years and are looking for different perspectives on the Pagan culture, this book is for all of us. Some of the material in this book will already be familiar to those of you with group experience, but I hope the rest of it will speak to all Pagans who live in a small town, came from a small town, or just want to know how 40 percent of us live our day-to-day spiritual lives.

I am only one Pagan living in one small town in America. I don't even come close to thinking I have all the answers. So in 2005 I came up with what I think was a fairly comprehensive survey about life as a small-town Pagan. Through the wonderful meetinghouse that is the Internet—LiveJournal (livejournal.com) and Witchvox, also known as the Witches' Voice (witchvox.com), specifically—I posted notices inviting interested parties to answer questions about everything from home décor to ritual attendance to child rearing.

I am blessed to have received fifty completed surveys, plus one interview via e-mail and four interviews via phone, about my subjects' specific cyber spiritual or first-time festival experiences. Some of the respondents are old friends I managed to guilt-trip into completing my survey or letting me interview them on specific topics; the rest I've gotten to know through working on this project. You will get to know them, too, as their comments and wisdom are quoted throughout the book in their own unique voices.

So if you think this book might be relevant to your living situation and your spiritual practice, I hope it is. I wrote it for you.

It also means you fall into one of the following three categories, which I call:

Hometowner

A *Hometowner* is someone who has grown up in a small town and discovered Paganism at some point or, like my daughter Rose, someone born into a Pagan family that lives in a small town. If you've never spoken face to face with another Pagan or attended a public ritual or other event in your life, I hope the information and encouragement from your fellow Hometowners in these pages will encourage you to do so.

Emigrant

An *Emigrant* is someone who grew up in a big city or suburb and has moved—or plans to move shortly—to a small town for career, love, health, or some other reason *after* starting to practice Paganism. While you probably have quite a good grasp of basic ritual and Pagan festival etiquette, you've probably had (or are afraid you will have) a bit of a culture shock in moving to a small town. I hope reading this will temper that shock somewhat, and reassure you that you are not the only former city-dweller who did something stupid (but thankfully not obviously stupid) while buying toilet paper in a small-town grocery store.

Interested researcher

You're curious about the reality of non-urban Pagan life in the early years of the twenty-first century and want to know more about it. All I can say is, the people who have already read the material in this book—both urban and small-town Pagans—think there's something in here for every one of us!

It is possible to be both a Hometowner and an Emigrant. I am. I grew up in a small town (population roughly 8,000 at the time). Looking back, I realize now that I was headed straight to Paganism, even as a teenager. The first clues were my inability to feel "spiritually fed" on Sunday mornings in the Episcopal church and my overwhelming sense of spiritual connection whenever I watched or performed the seasonal folk dances of England that were very popular in my hometown. However, I spent most of my twenties and thirties living somewhere in the Wilmington, Delaware / Baltimore, Maryland / Washington, DC corridor, and "discovered I was Pagan" while I was there. As of this writing, I share my town with the 4,400 other residents of Baldwin City, on the Kansas prairie—but I'm less than an hour away from all the Pagan amenities that Kansas City has to offer. By my standards, it's a pretty cool place to be Pagan.

What you hold in your hands looks and feels like a book. It even reads like a book. I don't like to think of it as a book, however; I prefer to see this object as a conversation. Imagine with me for a moment that you and I and the fifty people who contributed their thoughts and opinions are sitting around a very large version of your kitchen table, drinking coffee (or tea) and eating homemade cookies that are still warm from the oven as we swap stories about what it's like to be Pagan in small-town America at the beginning of the twenty-first century.

When you've finished this book, I hope you will gather together some local Pagans and invite them all to a restaurant or meeting space in your town for coffee, tea, warm cookies—and a continuation of our conversation.

CHAPTER 1

Popularity Contest

My parents weren't happy at first, but as time went on and they saw I was still me, not some weird girl wearing all black and sacrificing animals, they mellowed. They were hippies though, and a bit more open-minded than most in this town. My extended family just refuses to talk about it at all. Although when my parents died earlier this year, my relatives were "kind" enough to send me pamphlets explaining why I'd be spending eternity burning in hell. I was a bit pissed off about that. My brothers have always been okay about it. They're like, "Whatever."

I have lost friends over it and some actually cross the
street when they see me coming, but overall I think
because I've been calling myself a Witch for so long
that people have just gotten used to it.

—EVY, BOLIVAR, NEW YORK (POPULATION 1,089)

When I first had the idea to write this book, there was a "re-ality" television program on the Country Music Television network (CMT) called *Popularity Contest*. The premise was: take ten people from large East or West Coast metropoli-tan areas and dump them in Vega, Texas (population 896). The contestants lived in the townspeople's homes, worked in their businesses, and America got to laugh at the contestants' attempts to cope with small-town life. The residents of Vega were able to vote one person off each week, and the winner got $100,000—half of which was to be shared with some or all of the residents or organizations in the town, as the win-ner saw fit.

Even by reality show standards, *Popularity Contest* was pretty lame; it was a onetime show that was never repeated, probably because as many people tuned in to laugh at the "backward" residents of Vega, Texas, as tuned in to laugh at the contestants. As a cautionary tale for Hometowners and Emigrants, however, the show was priceless. The contestants and the residents learned some profound and relevant les-sons about tolerance and debunking stereotypes that you can apply to your own situation.

For example, the contestants on *Popularity Contest* were asked to go on a town-wide scavenger hunt their first day.

One of the items on the "to find" list was Devil's Rope, more commonly known as barbed wire, only they weren't told that. While the joke was on the contestants—how can anyone not know what barbed wire is?—the real test was in how they handled the joke. Some were angry, while others took it with grace and basic good humor—and were voted off much later than their more judgmental fellows. While there may not be $100,000 on the line in your situation, judging your fellow small-town residents by your newly discovered Pagan sensibilities and/or urban standards is just going to get you into trouble. My survey respondents agree.

So how do you fit in in a town you don't fit into? For Hometowners, this is a particularly difficult question, because up until you realized or decided you were Pagan, you probably fit in pretty well. And, unlike most people who reside in big cities, you are more likely to live near your family and childhood friends. You also see them more often as you go about your daily work, errands, and other activities than someone who lives in a city with a million other people. What do you do?

To Tell or Not to Tell: Coming Out of the Closet

We talk about "coming out of the broom closet" as Pagans much as gay men and lesbians talk about "coming out of the closet" about their sexuality, and if you're reading this and you're gay *and* Pagan in a small town, you most certainly have some big challenges ahead. I hope some of the advice in here will help make those mountainous challenges a little smaller. Lars, a gay Pagan friend who lives in a large East Coast city, reminded me recently, "You do not come out of any closet once and are done with it. You choose every day and with every person to be out or not."

> *Some family members suspect, but I haven't come right out and told them, and a few friends know. Because our area is very narrow-minded, I am not blatant about my religion, but if someone asked, I would tell them.*
>
> —KELTASIA, SHAMOKIN, PENNSYLVANIA (POPULATION 7,361)

The first and biggest question, of course, is whether to tell your family and friends about your religious identity. I can't tell you whether you should or not; no one can, because no one but you knows your family that well, understands your work relationships, or wants to keep your kids at the end of the messy divorce you may currently be going through.

I grew up in Berea, Kentucky, in the 1970s; the population at the time was about eight thousand. I moved away in high school and realized I was a Pagan while in college in Baltimore, Maryland. But up until I was in my mid-thirties, I returned to my hometown every Christmas, and always hid my Pagan identity from the people who'd known me the longest. I was convinced they wouldn't understand.

I joined Facebook about a year ago and have connected with 177 people as of this writing, at least half of whom I knew as a child and/or in high school—including my first ex-husband who even admitted on his own Facebook page that he left me because I was a Witch.[2] My profile, updates, and many of my posted notes leave no doubt in anyone's mind that I'm Pagan. As near as I can tell, no one cares. Of course, they haven't seen me in person since 1998, which is the last time I visited Berea; my reception may be very different face to face.

> *I have contact with friends since my parents still live in my hometown. My family is very supportive. In fact my mother "outed" me at a family reunion and I wasn't even there. No one has given me any negativity over being a Witch. My friends think it's pretty cool.*
>
> —K, SEVIERVILLE, TENNESSEE (POPULATION 17,297)

No matter where we live, some of us just don't have the freedom to say, "If my friends and family can't accept my beliefs it's their problem, not mine, so I won't hide who I am," as Deanna Eberlin of Addison, New York (population 1,708), wrote in her survey. I have heard story after story about bosses who say (or at least imply), "Come to my church or you're fired," and I'll bet you Hometowners have, too. Maybe it's even happened to you. Your friends might want to be supportive, but who knows how much pressure they're under from their own family, employers, and significant others to

---

2. And, yes, it was weird to read that, even though we've been casual friends for years.

drop you like a hot rock now that you're different? If you come out, you run a very big risk of being, at minimum, ostracized from the people you've known since kindergarten.

> *My family knows what I am, and for the most part*
> *have disowned me; they think I'm going to hell and*
> *taking my child with me.*
> —SPIRITRUNNER, BAKERSFIELD, CALIFORNIA
> (POPULATION 324,463), PREVIOUSLY IN TAFT,
> CALIFORNIA (POPULATION 9,032)

On the other hand, if you're living in the same small town you grew up in, don't underestimate your family's ability—and your friends' ability—to adapt and understand. No, not everyone will understand and accept your religion; hard or painful as that may be, it's part of the reality of being "different." But I think, and most of my survey respondents think, that you could be pleasantly surprised. Moondancer, from a small town in the state of Washington, agrees:

> *My family was well aware of my Pagan beliefs, al-*
> *though most of them don't understand any of it.*
> *The majority of them are Christian of one denomi-*
> *nation or another. There are a lot of Baptists in my*
> *family, as well as Assembly of God and other evan-*
> *gelical churches. I like to think that it doesn't affect*
> *my relationship with any of them; I still get sent all*
> *of the "inspirational" e-mails and sob stories from*
> *them that they send to all the other relatives, and*

while I occasionally wish there were some Pagan equivalents, for the most part I just smile, and accept the well-wishes for that and ignore the subcontext.

The few friends I have who are not Pagan are from work, and as I don't consider religion/spirituality to be appropriate to be discussed in the workplace, it rarely comes up.

Having said that, I don't make any particular attempt to hide or disguise my beliefs, and if asked directly, I'll answer with as much accuracy as I think they can handle.

I particularly like Moondancer's points about religion not being a particularly appropriate topic to discuss at work—unless you happen to work in a church, and about only giving your loved ones as much information as you think they can handle.[3] I have found, and many of my survey respondents have found, that a little at a time is best—kind of like how parents teach their children about sex: a little at a time over the years, and never more than they are ready to know. In other words, when you're at the next family reunion, don't dump the whole thing on your nice Methodist Aunt Virginia at once—that the God may or may not have antlers, horns, or cloven feet; the history of human sacrifice; the May First sex holiday known as Beltane. Show some tact, take it slow.

---

3. There will be more discussion about Paganism in the small-town work environment in chapter 8.

> *My parents thought it was a phase for a while, but*
> *now they accept it. The rest of my family accepts it.*
> *Though at first my little brother said I was going*
> *to hell, but then he read up on it and is probably a*
> *little bit Pagan too. Even my mom thinks she was*
> *a Native American medicine woman in a past life.*
>
> —KATHLEEN, FROM A TOWN IN NORTH DAKOTA

Your neighbors, too, may have questions about your faith once they notice your car is still in the driveway every Sunday morning or the odd nail-filled glass bottle hanging from a tree in your front yard. While fences do, in fact, make good neighbors, Julia and K both found that a few favors and a casual attitude about Paganism on your part go a long way toward making tolerant neighbors. Julia's advice in particular is something we can all take to heart, Emigrants and Hometowners alike:

> *Most of my neighbors get to know who I am before*
> *they find out about my religious practices. For the*
> *most part, my experiences have all been very posi-*
> *tive. We tend to help folks with shoveling the walk*
> *in the winter, the little old lady with the garbage,*
> *and stuff like that, so we are good neighbors. My*
> *religion is rarely mentioned at all, and it has not*
> *been negative at all here.*
>
> —JULIA, EAST STROUDSBURG,
> PENNSYLVANIA (POPULATION 10,411)

> *I have not shared my religious beliefs with too many*
> *people locally, especially as I am a relative new-*
> *comer. The few that I have told were either inter-*
> *ested in knowing what Paganism entailed or they*
> *just said, "Oh, okay" and left it at that. It has been*
> *a pleasant surprise for me to find this attitude in a*
> *highly Baptist area.*
>
> —K, SEVIERVILLE, TENNESSEE

Sometimes your neighbors may figure it out without you having to say or do a thing. And sometimes, as herbalist Witch of the Woods found out, your non-Pagan neighbors can actually actively help you in your spiritual practice.

> *The elderly couple across the street must know*
> *something, since the wife has many wild herbs*
> *I've used for medicine on her property. Once she*
> *stopped me and said I could dig up and transplant*
> *any herb I wanted for my "potions." She and her*
> *husband have been nothing but curious and sweet.*
> *Honestly, it's boring, but I have never had a nega-*
> *tive reaction, especially once people talk to me and*
> *ask me questions.*
>
> —WITCH OF THE WOODS, MERRIMAC,
> WISCONSIN (POPULATION 882)

Fitting In

Like the contestants on *Popularity Contest*, you may have a hard time fitting in if you're an Emigrant—partly because you're Pagan and partly because you're not used to small-town life. Even if there is a small Pagan presence in your town, if you're not careful you could still ruin your chances of social acceptance not only in the community at large, but also within your own "tribe."

> *Try not to sound like a "know-it-all" by saying, "This is how my group(s) used to do it." Everyone hates that, I think. I let them get to know me before offering authoritative opinions. Avoid asking "why," which is confrontational, and never say, "You should/ought . . ." People hate that, too. It sounds parental.*
>
> —ROWEN BRIANNA, BOWLING GREEN, KENTUCKY (POPULATION 56,598)

I was living in the suburbs of Washington, DC in 1999 when I fell in love with one of my oldest friends who was in graduate school in Columbia, Missouri (population currently 102,324). Even though I'd grown up in a small town, I had a genuine case of culture shock when I moved to the Midwest to be with him. For those of you who always hope for romantic endings, he'd been in love with me for about a decade at that point. We married in early 2001 and are still happily together.

I moved to a small town for love and had the hardest time fitting in—and not only because I was Pagan. Ironically, I'd been calling upon the four directions as part of my spiritual practice since 1985, and quickly realized I had trouble coping in a culture where people told you how to get somewhere by saying, "Turn north at . . . then turn west at . . ." I'd say, "Is that left or right?" and I'd get a funny look followed by a patient sigh and "It's north. Then west." I got lost fairly often that first year. Actually, ten years later I can still get lost if someone gives me directions based solely on, well, the directions.

One day I had only a few minutes before I was due somewhere else (either work or rehearsal for a play I was helping out with), and I *had* to stop at a grocery store and buy toilet paper. I looked at the posted store directory above the aisles and didn't see it listed, so I asked an employee where the toilet paper was. He said, "It's on the north wall." Like I was supposed to know instinctively which wall was the north wall! Of course it was the fourth wall I checked. Had I grown up with a more practical, non-ritual sense of the four directions, I probably wouldn't have been late for wherever I was headed.

I also talked too fast—like anyone from a large East Coast city would, which tended to alienate me from Pagans and non-Pagans alike. I'm still trying to break myself of this habit. It was also hard, with my semi-traditional Wiccan background and festival coordinator experience (I was one of the founders and was festival coordinator for several of the first ten Free Spirit Gatherings in Maryland), not to come across like a snob to my fellow small-town Pagans, most of whom had never been to a festival and had never had any formal religious training. I wish I'd had the following advice when I was trying to fit in:

> *It's not so much that I try to fit in, but I'm not into ad-*
> *vertising my Paganism. I might wear something very*
> *discreet (like a small pentacle), but that's about it.*
> —NOEY, COUPEVILLE, WASHINGTON (POPULATION 1,869)

Other respondents who didn't want to be quoted mentioned repeatedly that getting involved in the community was a good way to fit in for both Emigrants and Hometowners alike. Many of them talked about organizations they volunteered with that were compatible with their Pagan values—the town's animal shelter or park clean-up group were cited as favorites. Others suggested getting involved with local activities like elections, theater groups, or clubs that revolve around your not-spiritual interests (ham radio, dog training, scrapbooking, gardening, home-brewing, etc.) as ways to relate to people in your community in a safe, non-threatening way.

My husband and I have a small child, so our family also participates in local, seasonal activities. We attend Memorial Day parades, street fairs, Fourth of July fireworks (a perennial favorite!), farmers' markets, fall festivals, and summer activities at the local library. My daughter is also actively involved in soccer and gymnastics. Freezing on the sidelines with the other parents as your kids vainly attempt to kick a

ball, or waiting in the wings together at the year-end gymnastics recital, are bonding rituals that equal anything I've
ever experienced in ritual or at a Pagan festival! We hope
to eventually make casual friends at these events, whether
they're Pagan or not. In the meantime, these activities keep
us from hiding in the house and make us feel like part of the
community. Witch of the Woods agrees with me:

> *Definitely get to know the people you live with. I*
> *often exchange desserts and herbal meds with them.*
> *These small towns love it when you get involved,*
> *even on a small level. They will respect you if you*
> *participate with them. Volunteer at Little League or*
> *just be kind and respectful of others.*
>
> —WITCH OF THE WOODS, MERRIMAC, WISCONSIN

Sometimes the community provides its own Pagan activity
without even realizing it. When we lived in Portales, New
Mexico (population 12,184), we were shocked to discover
that seniors at the local high school had been winding ribbons around a Maypole during graduation week since 1929.

Ironically, the annual Maypole is the only dance event allowed on school property. The homecoming dance and se-
nior prom must be held at another location—usually at the
local college's gym—because the school board thinks those
other dances are "licentious." If only they knew!

The yearly high school Maypole Dance is a big event in the
community—the public is invited and the auditorium is packed.
Parents and grandparents attend the final dress rehearsal to film

and photograph the event. The boys wear tuxedos and the girls wear formal full-length dresses, complete with hoop skirts. The couples weave the ribbons, and then waltz around the pole. I'm considered to be somewhat of an expert on the history of Maypole dancing and am full of advice on how to make and dance around one, but even I would not try to do the Maypole in a hoop skirt![4] I have no idea how the girls manage.

The *Portales News-Tribune* faithfully covers the event every year; this is front-page news. An article in the May 22, 2005, edition of the *News-Tribune* spends several column inches on the dresses and how several generations of the same families have danced around the Maypole, but only briefly touches on the Maypole itself:

> *Maypole is historically a fertility and pagan* [sic] *ritual, but at PHS* [Portales High School], *it has become like a second prom for graduating seniors, only much more formal. The original intention of the dance does not seem to sway participants . . .*[5]

Of course, not every small-town high school conveniently provides a Maypole dance for the community at graduation time, but if you look hard enough, you're bound to find a local activity or custom that feeds your Pagan soul.

---

4. See the "Spring" chapter in my book *Make Merry in Step and Song: A Seasonal Treasury of Music, Mummer's Plays & Celebrations in the English Folk Tradition* (Llewellyn, 2009).

5. Helena Rodriguez, "Maypole to Unwind at High School." Online at http://www.pntonline.com/news/maypole-4986-phs-prewitt.html.

Slow, Subtle, and Quiet is the Way to Go

When my husband A.G. was an undergraduate at a major state university (the culture of which can very much resemble a small- to medium-sized town), the girlfriend of one of his closest friends decided to become a Witch and out herself to the entire university community at the same moment. There's an old theory that if you say, "I'm a Witch" three times while turning in place, you'll instantly be one. However, the young lady chose to conduct this rite of passage at full volume, in ritual robes, in the middle of a very crowded student cafeteria at lunchtime.

You probably already know that this is not the best way to reveal your religious preferences in a small town, but just in case there's any doubt, my survey respondents would probably copy A.G.'s reaction to the spontaneous self-initiation in the cafeteria and laugh uproariously—and he already knew he was Pagan at the time. Maybe the young lady should have heeded the following counsel:

> *I'd offer a bit of advice from the so-called "long version" of the Rede of the Wicca: "Soft of eye and light of touch—speak little, listen much." Take pride in yourself, but you don't need to beat your friends and neighbors over the head with your religion or spirituality. At the same time, pick your battles—not everything is worth fighting over, but some things are. It's a tough choice sometimes to know which is which.*
>
> —MOONDANCER, WASHINGTON STATE

Consider why you want to tell various people—do they need to know? Do you just want to get it off your chest, or do you just want to be in their face about it? This doesn't have to be a public issue, but on the other hand, being in the broom closet carries its own special risk. If you live in a "right to work" state, then your employer can fire you for any reason not against the law—they don't like your clothes, for example. Even though religious discrimination is against the law, another excuse is easy to come up with and lawyers are very expensive. See Dana D. Eilers's book Pagans and the Law.[6]

—ROWEN BRIANNA, BOWLING GREEN, KENTUCKY

Rowen Brianna brings up an interesting point about the motive for letting those around you know about your religious beliefs. Maybe you do want to "just be in their face" and would do just about anything to shock your family, friends, and neighbors out of their presumed small-town conservative outlook—and I say "presumed," because in my experience there is a much stronger "live and let live" mentality in small-town residents than city-dwellers give us credit for.

There are places from one extreme all the way to the other in terms of acceptance of Pagans. A place

---

6. Dana D. Eilers, *Pagans and the Law: Understand Your Rights* (Career Press, 2009).

> *known for its wide acceptance isn't always better*
> *than a tiny town known for its Christian population.*
> —BECCA, CLOVIS, NEW MEXICO (POPULATION 32,863)

Let me give you an example. I was once staffing a vending booth at a Pagan festival about an hour from my home here in Kansas, when one of the merchants in a nearby booth realized that he and his boothmates needed some additional food and drink supplies to get them through the rest of the weekend. He decided he needed to make a Walmart run. The nearest Walmart to the festival was in the big town up the road from mine, population about 80,000.

Now, this gentleman had been wearing very little except a thigh-length leopard-print nylon bathrobe all weekend, and did he change clothes for his Walmart run? He did not. Was he beaten up, laughed at, insulted, or refused service at the local Walmart? He was not. Heck, his picture didn't even end up on www.peopleofwalmart.com (yes, I checked). He probably would have done better to take Julia and Noey's advice, however:

> *Don't shove your religion in people's faces. Most*
> *people are not going to have a problem with your*
> *spirituality as long as you don't push it on them.*
> *If these people have known you your whole life and*
> *know who you are, it's probably not going to change*

> much, unless you have been obnoxious or have a
> chip on your shoulder.
>
> —JULIA, EAST STROUDSBURG, PENNSYLVANIA

> Find something discreet to wear; once folks get used
> to that and get to know you, move slowly into more
> direct forms of expression but always remember:
> We are the Hidden Children.
>
> —NOEY, COUPEVILLE, WASHINGTON

On the other hand, it's hard to live a lie as, again, many gay men and lesbians can attest to, to pretend you're a bona fide member of the "mainstream" (whatever that is) when you know in your heart that you're not. It's tough to censor yourself constantly so you don't inadvertently out yourself to friends or co-workers.

I've been calling myself Pagan for over two decades now, and I still have trouble keeping certain phrases out of my vocabulary when I'm not in Pagan company. I frequently slip up and say things like "Oh, Goddess" instead of "Oh, God" (or "My God"), and "Godsdammit" often pops out of my mouth when I'm annoyed or frustrated. Occasionally I will use the expletive "Sweet Buddha's tits" which is at least a little less religiously inflammatory (except maybe to Buddhists). I've even been known to recount time based on Pagan holidays to non-Pagans, as in "Yes, Mr. Mechanic, I know my car was supposed to have the oil changed sometime back around Lammas." Oops.

Since my early Pagan days in 1985, I've had very few friends who weren't Pagan, and none of them were what I'd consider close friends—more like good acquaintances. These few friends may have thought we were close, but I knew better. If they didn't know I was Pagan, it was probably because I'd determined they couldn't accept that I wasn't Christian, which meant our entire friendship was based on a lie. You may already be doing the same thing, and if you are, you know how lonely, painful, and yet occasionally necessary this choice can be.

In addition, you may initially have a positive coming-out experience with your family, and then realize years later—usually during a crisis—that they've never really accepted your religion at all. This happened to us. A.G. told his mother sometime in the late 1980s that he was Pagan. Did she ask what that meant or offer to pray for his misguided soul? No. She just asked him if he'd still come home for Thanksgiving and Christmas dinners—these two meals being the most important rites on my mother-in-law's ecumenical calendar. The holidays these feasts are attached to mean almost nothing to her; it's all about the family getting together and eating well. Once he reassured her that he'd still come home for the sacred suppers, she completely lost interest in his religious identity. She told the rest of the family; no one ever said anything negative to A.G.—or to me, after we were married—and we assumed all was well with our religion and his blood kin and that was the end of the issue.

We were wrong. In the late summer of 2003, A.G.'s father was dying of blood cancer. He'd been unplugged from some of the life-support machines when A.G. and I went into his intensive care unit room to say goodbye. My father-in-law wanted to let go, and had specifically asked to be taken off the machines. He and A.G. were cracking jokes, and A.G. asked me to sing something for his father. I started to sing an old English folk song I'd sung in front of my devout Methodist grandmother on more than one occasion—in other words, I was not singing anything particularly "Witchy." A.G.'s older sister was in the room at the time, yelled out "Freaks!" and stormed out. By the time I'd finished the song and we left the room, rumors were flying all over the packed family waiting area that I was "practicing Witchcraft" on my father-in-law in the middle of the ICU. Needless to say, this caused a rift in the family that is still healing seven years later.

The problem is, if you've grown up in a small town and have recently discovered your Pagan leanings, it's too late to avoid non-Pagan family and good friends. Not only do you probably have a handful of really good non-Pagan friends, but these people have also been your friends for years. You also have nearby family to consider. And now your friends and family may hate you for "changing the rules" on them, for changing your perspective as you study more and more about your new path. If there is a situation with more potential for pain in small-town Pagan life, I can't think of it.

Fortunately, my surveyed experts had a lot of advice about balancing coming out of (or staying in) the broom closet with being true to yourself—especially for Hometowners:

Don't go out of your way to announce it, but don't be afraid to be who you are. And you better be strong in what you believe because you will be constantly challenged.

However, there are a lot of people who are in the closet here and don't want any spotlight shown on them. They come to me with lots of questions and advice; it's kind of funny to watch people be that way, but I don't mind. I do have some bumper stickers on my Explorer that indicate it belongs to a non-Christian and have had "Witch" scratched into the hood of my truck!

—JENN, MOUNTAIN HOME,
IDAHO (POPULATION 12,266)

Be the same person you always were. Unless you were an asshole, then you might want to change, but my point is, if people see that you aren't just trying to freak them out, that this is still just you, they'll be more accepting.

Most often people just ask about my necklace (it's a small pentacle) and then move on. I've been pretty lucky: most have been pretty good about it, but occasionally I've been handed pamphlets and told I'm going to burn in hell. A pizza shop owner once refused to serve me because of my necklace, and I refused to remove it.

—EVY, BOLIVAR, NEW YORK

> *People in small towns are just . . . skittish when it comes to differences. Ease them into it. Don't go running through town dressed like a hippie, doused in patchouli, yelling, "Long live the sun god, he's a real fun god! RA! RA! RA!" Don't go out into your backyard buck nekkid waving your athame at the stars. Cops will probably be called, even if you truly are on your own property and can do what you please. Keep it low-key, unless you really, really like stirring up the neighborhood.*

—RAVENNA, DOWAGIAC, MICHIGAN, (POPULATION 5,635)

Advice for the Stranger in a Strange Land: The Emigrant

I've been away from the East Coast for over a decade now, and I have the strong Midwesterner identity to prove it—with one exception: after living near New York City-style pizza and/or with former New Yorkers who were raised on New York City-style pizza (thin crust with cheese that is likely to slide off with no warning whatsoever) for so many years, I still fold my pizza slice in half lengthwise before I eat it. This is pretty hard to do with thick, Midwestern, Chicago-style crusts, but I manage!

I also fold toast, quesadilla slices, and anything else that's flat and doesn't need a fork to eat. I can't help it; I don't even do it consciously. The funny thing is, people here in the Midwest (not to mention my husband, who has never lived on the East Coast) tend to stare at me more for my "food-folding" than they do my Celtic knotwork T-shirts or crescent-moon jewelry. Other than "Don't fold your food," here's what my respondents had to say to Emigrants who have recently moved to a small town:

> *Don't pay attention to the criticism, but don't go trying to convert people either. When people are ready to discover a new truth, they will seek you out.*
>
> —JENN, MOUNTAIN HOME, IDAHO

> *Take a deep breath, slow down, and learn to amuse yourself. It's pretty quiet here, though there are plenty of opportunities to get out and just be with nature.*
>
> —BECCA, CLOVIS, NEW MEXICO

> *Don't try to flaunt being a Pagan; don't assume the town is out to get you; don't assume we don't like you because you're Pagan—it could be your personality, after all!*
>
> —NOEY, COUPEVILLE, WASHINGTON

> *Don't make a big deal out of it. Confrontation helps nobody. If a particular person is supposed to know, an occasion will arise.*
>
> —DONNA HAMES, NASHWAUK,
> MINNESOTA (POPULATION 960)

CHAPTER 2

Making Contact

I go to Boise (about 50 miles away) at least once a week to Crone's Cupboard, because my mentor is there. I really love to soak up the energy of the shop and the wonderful people you meet there are great! I also plan to go to Washington next year for the Spring Mysteries, not to mention the yearly trip to GoddessFest.

—JENN, MOUNTAIN HOME, IDAHO

Hometowners, you can certainly choose to stay solitary and never speak to another Pagan face to face if you want to. By my definition, religion is what you do with other people, but spirituality is between you and the Gods. Likewise, Emigrants who have had enough Pagan community contact and politics and stupidity and petty bickering and backstabbing to last several lifetimes may appreciate the solitude and personal spiritual focus that life in a small town and away from most, if not all, other Pagans can provide.

That being said, there are definitely advantages to being in at least semi-regular contact with other members of the Pagan community. The best reason to sit in a formal or informal circle with others once in a while is the opportunity for some basic reality checks. Are you grounding and centering properly? Are you really in a trance state on a guided meditation, or are you just daydreaming—or asleep? If you have only done ritual by yourself, you are much more vulnerable to imaginary spiritual experiences.

Let me give you an example. At one time, my coven offered holiday rituals that were open to the community. A solitary came to one of our Beltane celebrations, speaking to anyone who would listen about her amazing psychic powers and her "astral fiancé." Apparently she'd met a man on the astral plane—but never in real life—and they planned to marry just as soon as she moved to Ireland and figured out which one of several hundred thousand Irishmen he was. To further hinder her search, she didn't even know his name. As an occasional writer of fiction, I wish I could make up stuff this good.

Does the idea of an anonymous "astral fiancé" sound a little far-fetched? It sure did to us—especially when she quit her job, moved to Ireland, and (no surprise) never found him. Last we heard she was back in the States, flat broke, and living out of her car. If this woman had had some solid training and/or regular contact with a group at the beginning of her Pagan studies, she'd have known better than to delude herself to the point of homelessness. Plus, she hadn't a clue that no one at our Beltane ritual cared one whit about her "amazing psychic powers," or that repeatedly boasting about your Gods-given talents is considered rude in polite Pagan company—but her rudeness in mentioning them (repeatedly) has stuck with us to this day.

There was also a woman in our local weekly discussion group when we lived in Wisconsin who had likewise never spent any time in a "mainstream" Pagan community, and as a result had some pretty set (but inaccurate) opinions about some of her fellow practitioners. The two I remember most were "all Gardnerians are into BDSM" (they're not) and "all Asa Tru [followers of the Norse deities] are white supremacists" (they're not). It took a long time for us to convince her, without alienating her, that she was, well, wrong. But if she'd just gone to one or two of the smaller events at Circle Sanctuary outside of Madison—about three hours away—she'd have been far less likely to develop these interesting notions.

Like Craves Like

It's human nature to want to join with and bond to "those like us," and Pagans are no exception to the rule.[7] Many of the survey respondents said that they'd had some limited contact with other Pagans in or near their small town, although some also reported problems of incompatibility:

> *I have attended an open circle, but while I liked the people in the group, we don't practice the same kind of Paganism.*
>
> —EVY, BOLIVAR, NEW YORK

> *There are about ten to twenty Pagans that I know of in my town, though I know there are more. I think the rest of them are solitary. I already belong to a group, and I have been in it since 2001. My group has a ritual once a month on the full moon; it's all very positive.*
>
> —KATHLEEN, FROM A TOWN IN NORTH DAKOTA

> *My contact with other Pagans here has been minimal. There was a brief encounter with a couple at the local bookstore—they were having a fun game of "make fun of the books being offered"—during which they pointed me in the direction of a monthly study group in a town down the road. I*

---

7. A full discussion of how to start your own discussion group, coven, or regular meetup is covered in chapter 7.

only attended one meeting, and by the time I had
settled in enough to try to attend another meeting
the shop had shut down, and I don't know what
happened to the members. I assume they went back
to their respective lives. Beyond those two encoun-
ters, nothing that I can recall.

—BECCA, CLOVIS, NEW MEXICO

There are just four others in my town that I'm
aware of. Last week a young girl at a "Family Fun"
night was proudly wearing a pentacle. It was nice
to see!

—IRIS, GENOA, ILLINOIS (POPULATION 5,145)

On the Road

In the survey, I asked, "Have you traveled to attend a Pagan event (open ritual, discussion group, gathering) or to visit a Pagan shop? Why or why not? How far did you travel? How often do you travel to do these things?" Unlike the Pagan residents of Washington, DC, or even Kansas City (and those cities' suburbs), most small-town Pagans don't have the luxury of Pagan events in their "backyard" so to speak, and must travel—sometimes hundreds of miles—in order to find people to talk to or circle with. I think, and I believe my survey respondents would agree with me, that it takes an extra level of commitment to the practice of your faith to pack up and drive two, three, four, or more hours (one way) in order to have any connection with your community at all.

Many survey respondents reported being willing to travel in order to connect with other Pagans, while others indicated that travel was prohibitive, either for financial or family reasons:

> *Our town is about a forty-five-minute drive from Seattle; however, we've gone across country to attend gatherings more than once. These days, unless it's for something specific to our Tradition of the Craft, we don't generally travel to attend. An exception this year is a long-running Pagan camping festival that we will be attending near the Columbia River Gorge, which we have not attended for the past several years due to timing.*
> —MOONDANCER, WASHINGTON STATE

> *I have attended a few Wiccan/Pagan rituals at a local metaphysical store about twenty miles from my home and have attended Native American ceremonies about an hour and a half from my home.*
> —KELTASIA, SHAMOKIN, PENNSYLVANIA

Keltasia brings up an interesting point: there may very well be activities in faiths not your own that are close enough to your house, and compatible enough with your beliefs, that they will at least somewhat feed you spiritually in between, or even in place of, attending rituals or other events with your fellow Pagans. For this reason, I have "hung out" on the fringes of the Buddhist community for over a decade; I've gone to retreats (and had to smuggle in my own non-vegetarian fare) and weekly meditations when there was nothing else available. I learned more about grounding and centering and the art of silently listening for Deity to speak to me—not that I'm good at that particular skill—sitting in meditation with Buddhists than I have at any one-time or regular Pagan event in my life.

> *I have traveled several hundred miles to be at events in the past. I don't do it so much these days, as I like staying home. It used to be we traveled to gatherings several times a year; now it's just a couple of times a year. I visit my Pagan shop and the other metaphysical shop in town at least twice a month. I prefer to buy from them because it keeps them in business.*
>
> —JULIA, EAST STROUDSBURG, PENNSYLVANIA

So if you do decide to travel outside of your hometown and/or comfort zone in order to attend a festival, workshop, or open ritual, what can you expect? What should you do? How should you behave?

For Emigrants, attending a festival or community ritual with or without knowing any other participants probably isn't that big a deal. In fact, if you're used to a certain amount of contact with your fellow Pagans, you may *need* to drive some distance to attend various Pagan events, stay active with the coven you left behind, or visit Pagan shops in order to continue to feel spiritually connected to the Divine and to your "tribe."

I went to a Witches' Ball once. That was fun. It was in Batavia, which is about an hour and a half away. I also went to an open circle, but it wasn't for me. I've been told there's a Pagan shop in Hornell, which is about forty minutes away, but no one seems to know exactly where it is. Why don't I go more often? I work constantly, and I don't really have anyone to go with. Starwood Pagan Festival isn't that far away, but again, I have no one to go with.

—EVY, BOLIVAR, NEW YORK

On the other hand, as Evy points out, Hometowners may feel an understandable amount of apprehension at the idea of driving some distance—often to the nearest big city—and interacting with a bunch of strangers who just happen to also call themselves "Pagan." It's scary—and it was scary for Emigrants to "step out" into Pagan society the first time, too. But there are benefits in even occasional face-to-face contact with others of a like mind, so try to get to at least one festival or open ritual a year. Your spirituality will be enriched by the experience, I promise. And hopefully you won't end up homeless and living out of your car because you were unable to find your astral soulmate in Ireland.

Basic Pagan Community Etiquette

So what do you need to know in order to fit in and not make too many major social blunders at an open ritual, workshop, or regular discussion group (also called a *moot*, *Pagan Night Out* or *PNO*, or *meetup*)? See, in many cases, the Pagan community has very different rules. Yes, we still say *please* and *thank you* and take hot showers (with soap!) on a regular basis—or at least we should—but there are some different rules that can be completely incomprehensible to newcomers and outsiders. Here are some of the big ones.

Outing

The primary rule for everyone in the community is: don't *ever* give out a Pagan's full name, contact information (including e-mail or cell-phone number), or work location without prior permission—*even to fellow Pagans*. This is called "outing," and it is just about the worst thing you can do to someone. If you meet someone who wants to contact your Pagan friend down the street, say, take the acquaintance's information (with permission) and give it to your friend when you get home. That gives her the option of giving her own contact information to your acquaintance. Several years ago, my husband A.G. had to sternly remind a Pagan friend of this basic etiquette point when the friend gave A.G.'s phone number to the local newspaper without checking with A.G. first. Graduate students don't like to be awakened at dawn on days they don't have classes, which is what this reporter did—he wanted the annual "interview a Witch for Halloween" story for the local paper.

Touching sacred objects

The next most important rule, and one that is so often un-thinkingly broken by novices is: don't touch someone else's "Witchy stuff" without their permission. This includes crystals, rocks, tarot cards, jewelry, robes or other ritual garb, familiars (pets who help you magically), and altar tools—especially athames (ritual knives). If the items are on display in the public part of the house you happen to be sitting in, it usually means the owner won't mind your touch, *but only if you ask first*. A good rule of thumb is to ask even when the owner is handing something to you.

For example: I recently attended a major Pagan festival where the land is very steep between the camping and merchant areas at the top of the ridge and the workshop sites and deity-specific groves—and food and hot showers—at the bottom of the ridge. I was taking the shuttle van back to the top of the property after lunch when some other riders got in. One of them handed me her newly purchased carved staff to hold while she climbed into the van seat in front of me. Even in that hurried, crowded, non-ritual moment, I asked, "May I?" before I touched it, even though she obviously wanted me to hold it for her. She said, "Of course," and I held it until she was settled in her seat, after which she reclaimed the staff and said, "Thank you," and we all went about our polite Pagan business.

If someone bestows upon you the very great honor of letting you near his or her personal altar, don't even *think* about touching anything on it. This is as true for public events like festivals as it is in someone's living room. Why? Because it's *their* altar, dedicated to *their* deity or deities, and you and your energy have no business blundering into their personal means of honoring and connecting to their God(s). It's kind of like the magical equivalent of going into someone else's home, turning on their computer without permission, and using it to check your e-mail. It's just not done.

Sure, you could make the argument, "Well, if they didn't want people touching their altar stuff, they shouldn't have it out in public space," and you would have a valid point. Unfortunately, in the Pagan community, you'd still be in the wrong to touch someone else's altar, just as you would their personal computer outside the Pagan community.

Please note that this also applies to temporary altars set up for a public or open ritual at a park or, say, the local Unitarian church. Even though the circle is not taking place in someone's "home space" like a living room or festival campsite, the officiants probably don't have two sets of ritual tools—one for private use and one for public use. Most only have one set, their personal set. Unless otherwise invited, leave it alone.

Now, if there is danger or hazard involved—the altar cloth has caught fire or the altar has been bumped and the ceramic Isis statue is headed for a fatal encounter with a cement floor, by all means step in if you are in close enough proximity to prevent loss or disaster. Put out the fire, save the High Priestess' favorite Isis statue now—and apologize profusely later.

Familiars and pets

In regards to familiars or other animals, always follow house rules. Katie is our pathologically shy dog—shy to the point that she will have a panic seizure if she becomes too stressed. Whenever we have open rituals in our home, we simply move Katie's crate (which she loves) to the spare bedroom and post a "Private: Do Not Enter" sign on the door. Once most of the people have gone home after the post-ritual feast, we'll let her out, but ask that people wait for her to approach them, and to please ignore her until or unless she initiates contact. Because of our strictly enforced rules, Katie has never had a seizure on ritual days. Of course it helps that guests who deliberately break Katie's rules aren't invited to return.

If you are afraid of or allergic to specific animals, check with the hosts if the ritual or workshop will be held in a private home to see if they have any pets on the property. Depending on the severity of your allergy or discomfort levels, you may want to reconsider attending the event. I've developed an allergy to rabbits in the last five years or so after a childhood filled with several instances of rescuing orphaned baby bunnies and raising them until they were old enough to be released back into the wild. It's annoying, but I can take over-the-counter antihistamine before I leave for a ritual where I know there will be lagomorphs, and I do just fine. However, if I knew the ritual at a rabbit-inclusive home was going to be particularly long, intense, or would involve a very long (quiet) pathworking or meditation, I'd probably stay home. Even with the antihistamine, I still sniffle and blow my nose a lot when I'm around rabbits for more than a couple of hours.

One of our dogs is a one-hundred-pound German shepherd who is a complete Goofbucket (our favorite nickname for him) and devoted to any child he meets, although he is standoffish with adults he doesn't know. Karl is harmless, but can look pretty scary—until you get his red rubber ball and offer to throw it for him; he loves his red rubber ball. We tell people up front that we have a huge dog who will bark until he gets to know them. This doesn't bother most first-time attendees, but some people have elected not to come to our home because they knew in advance they wouldn't be able to set aside their fear of large dogs enough to fully experience the ritual or concentrate on the workshop. We respect that.

I, on the other hand, am stark raving teleport-to-another-room-if-one's-loose-in-the-house freaking terrified of bats. I know for a fact that if someone had a pet bat I would never, ever be able to attend a ritual at that person's house. I've had bats loose in my home and found myself outside on the front lawn a second or two after seeing the bat fly at me—with absolutely no memory of actually running down the stairs and out the front door. I. Do. Not. Like. Bats. Fortunately for my psyche, not too many people, not even Pagans, keep bats as pets.

And by all that is sacred and holy, just because your spirit animal or totem animal just happens to be the same species or breed of an animal that belongs to another Pagan, don't assume for one second that you have any rights to talk to, touch, or otherwise interact with that animal without the owner's permission. I see this most often with Pagans who have raptors or other birds of prey as spirit or totem animals who think just because a presenter or fellow attendee brings their personal hunting hawk or a barn owl they're trying to rehabilitate (because it's part of their day job) to an event or ritual, the Pagan with the hawk or crow totem is *entitled* to touch, hold, pet, or otherwise "take over" that animal.

Once a fellow presenter—and licensed raptor rescuer—at a Pagan festival brought a crow she'd recently acquired with her for the weekend because it needed extra care. The crow had been living with humans since shortly after birth; there was no way the bird could ever be released into the wild. She was a friendly bird, but that did not give this one attendee who babbled and hinted all weekend about her personal "crow energy" any right to constantly pester my fellow attendee to let her hold and/or adopt the poor crow.

I've also seen this behavior with people who feel spiritually connected to snakes and ferrets, but the bird-of-prey-as-totem-animal people are the worst. Unless you are specifically invited, leave the animal alone. And if you *are* invited to touch or hold the animal, treat it *exactly* as you would someone else's ritual athame and be reverent, respectful, and follow the owner's instructions exactly. I did, and got to hold a lovely red-tailed hawk on my wrist one day as a result. My totem animal is the stag, but it was still a big spiritual thrill to hold that hawk.

Tolerance

At some point in our lives, we've all heard the Golden Rule: treat others as you yourself would like to be treated. Now that you're a Pagan, this rule still applies to you. Don't judge, gossip about, or be rude to someone just because he or she belongs to a different category of people from you or for some personal trait over which he or she has no control. This includes gender or sexual orientation, health conditions, age, weight or lack thereof (thin people hurt when teased, too), race or place of origin, and dietary choices—vegan, vegetarian, *or* meat-eater.

Here are some general etiquette points guaranteed to minimize becoming a hot news item on Pagan Gossip Central if you follow them:

- Politely avoid people you disagree with or feel are emotional or spiritual "bullies."

- Saying "You are more powerful than I am" is a good way to not be taken seriously.

- Saying "I am more powerful a Witch than you" is *really* rude.

- There is more than one right way to practice Paganism. If it doesn't cause nonconsensual bodily harm or exploit minors, leave it be.

- Don't cut down other peoples' Gods.

- There is more than one way to do ritual. Some are quiet and meditative, which, if you've been working for a long time as a solitary, are probably what you're most accustomed to. Other rituals involve dancing, drumming, and screaming. Both are acceptable, and meet certain needs at certain times.

All of the above is just to prevent you from making some of the most common newcomers' faux pas. One final note: you are expected to follow these basic tolerance rules on the Internet, too.

Just because you're Pagan, it doesn't mean you have to be so open-minded about any ideas that your brain falls out the back of your head. If it hurts someone, especially someone helpless (like children), it's wrong. If it's based on a television show, a novel or a movie, it's silly (look up Klingon Wicca or Jedi Wicca the next time you're on the Internet). If you're "borrowing" folk customs or magics from another culture, get your facts straight—otherwise you're going to end up looking like a complete idiot.

Let me give you an example. I know a gentleman who believes himself to be a German Witch. He calls himself a *Hexer* and goes on and on at great length on various online forums about how German *Hexerei* and *Strega* (Italian Witchcraft) are the same thing; they're not. To prove his point, this guy regularly posts pictures of his ritual spoon—a wooden spoon that he's carved himself and covered with runes.[8]

My German mother-in-law has a carved spoon with a decorative fabric bow tied just above the bowl. It hangs on the wall of her informal dining room, and its function is to bring prosperity to her house. Her ritual spoons are the ones

---

8. Just how this is supposed to prove his point, I have no clue.

she uses to stir her sacred pot of boiling potatoes and they are quite plain-looking. I've talked with a few people who practice Strega, and they all tell me that the ritual spoon in their tradition is the one their grandmother uses to stir the sacred marinara sauce—and that these spoons were also quite plain-looking. Hmm, maybe Strega and Hexerei have more in common than we thought! (Just kidding!)

Basic ritual etiquette

Nine times out of ten, if you're the guest at a group's ritual or attending a public circle in a nearby town, someone will make a point of thoroughly explaining the ritual beforehand, usually the High Priest or High Priestess or one of the other officiants. You may even be assigned a "mentor," an experienced ritualist you can sit next to and mimic (if necessary) during the actual rite. There are, however, some basic courtesies that are common enough to be useful in just about any circle.

Unless okayed during the pre-circle talk-through (and it's considered good manners to ask if it isn't mentioned), do not leave the defined ritual space—i.e., a cast circle—without permission, and then only in an emergency. A sudden need to go to the bathroom is an emergency. Answering or texting on your cell phone—which you should have turned off and left in the other room anyway—is not an emergency unless a close family member is on the verge of death or is about to give birth. And if someone that close to you is in either condition, you probably have somewhere better to be than in a room full of relative strangers—like the hospital, perhaps.

If you need to leave the ritual space, whisper this information to your "mentor," who is probably sitting next to you. He or she will know what to do, whether to ritually "let you out" themselves or get someone more in charge to do so. Wait until he or she "cuts a gate" in the cast circle before you leave, and then wait until he or she cuts another one to let you back in.

Why is this such a big deal? Well, some groups believe that a ritually defined space helps channel and direct the flow of psychic energy raised during the rite. If you just get up and walk out, it's as if you just poked a hole in a kiddie pool full of water. The energy drains away. If you are in circle with a group like that and you "poke a hole" in their sacred space, don't expect to be invited back. Ever.

Other groups work on the theory that very small children and pets can pass through the barrier of the ritual space without disrupting the energy. If you're reading this, you're probably neither a very small child nor a pet, so make sure you follow group protocol.

You are a guest. You are not the High Priest or High Priestess. This means that your main job is to not do or say anything unless it is indicated that your spontaneous contribution would be acceptable. One joke or smart-ass remark at the wrong time is (a) disrespectful, (b) rude, and (c) disruptive. If you cared enough about your own spiritual journey to attend this ritual in the first place, why ruin it for everyone else? I was a guest at a Beltane ritual a couple years ago, and unfortunately could not get away from another guest who just had to make a smart or snarky comment at every part of the ritual. I wasn't in charge—it wasn't my place to tell her to shut the hell up or kick her out—but it definitely lessened my enjoyment of the ritual.

Part of the rite very well may involve shared food, drink, peace pipe, etc. Of course, if you're recovering from a cold, be polite and don't contaminate everyone else. And whatever you do, don't refuse to partake outright without an explanation (and the explanation had better be a good one!), or your refusal will be seen as an insult.

Otherwise, if you can accept the offering as a whole, do so. It is a great honor to have been included in the sharing. If you can accept the energy of the substance, but not the substance itself, do so with respect. This is usually an issue if wine or mead is being passed around and, for whatever reason (you're pregnant, you're a recovering alcoholic, you're underage and don't want to get your host(s) in trouble, you're on antibiotics, etc.), you feel you cannot safely partake. Salute or otherwise go through the motions. Discussing this with the ritual leader beforehand would be an even better idea. He or she may already know how to handle this situation and will instruct you. If for some reason you can't accept either the energy of the offering or the actual food or drink, don't. Bow in respect, politely pass it on, and consider not circling with this particular group again.

In general, remember that you are, in fact, in a place of worship. A place of worship that holds deep meaning for someone. It probably looks, feels, and sounds nothing like where you do your personal rituals at home, but it—and the people gathered there—still merit your respect.

What about sex?

Good question!

Throughout history, Pagans and Witches have been accused of engaging in orgies, sexual overindulgences, and general licentious behavior that would shock a sacred prostitute. Public perception today is about what it was five hundred years ago—and there's some truth to it. As of this writing, I have been invited to an orgy, given the opportunity to play Naked Twister, and flat-out asked if I wanted to have sex with someone not my mutually monogamous husband within the past week (granted, I was at a Pagan gathering, but still . . .). I said, "No, thank you" to all of the above; it's okay to say "No."

If/when you venture out into Pagan public, chances are good someone will ask you to have sex with them. You may even want to ask someone to have sex with you. Since our standards of good behavior—i.e. sexual mores—are slightly different from those of the general public, how do you handle it?

Believe it or not, the Pagan community does have some basic sexual protocols based on two very important virtues: honesty and respect. Knowing these protocols, and sticking to them, will definitely save your good reputation—and could save your life.

Pagans, being on the religious "fringe" of society, tend to attract people who are on the "fringe" in other areas as well—including sexually. This means that we can be, and often are, heterosexual, bisexual, homosexual, celibate, trisexual, meta-sexual, pansexual, intersexual, asexual, and transgendered. We also attract, because we *tolerate* (very important), people who are sexually into leather, chocolate, barbed wire, rubber, uniforms, general nudity, and polka music. If one or more of the above makes you uncomfortable, start practicing your polite poker face now.

Where do Pagans draw the line sexually? Same as the rest of Western society: nonconsensual sex, adults having sex with children, and anyone having sex with animals. Other than that, pretty much anything between consenting adults is fine with us.

As I mentioned, a "no" answer is always a valid response to an unwanted sexual advance. If you don't want to sleep with someone, say so! If the person persists, tell somebody. Better yet, tell *lots* of somebodies. Anyone who will not accept a polite "no" and attempts to use coercion deserves to be expelled from the community.

If a person you're not interested in propositions you, be polite. For some reason, this happens to my husband a lot. He is straight, but he is a "daddy bear," and therefore very attractive to a certain percentage of gay men who like their partners big, fuzzy, and with distinguishing gray hair at the temples. His response to unwelcome propositions is always this: "Thank you, I'm very flattered, but I'm straight." Because he was polite, some of the men who've propositioned him over the years are now numbered among his best friends.

Polyamorous relationships in which one or both parties are allowed "outside" sexual encounters are very common in the Pagan community, and usually follow one of two basic rules. The first is "two for one." Say Leah and Wolf are married, and Willow is interested in having sex with Wolf. Under the two for one rule, Willow had better be bisexual, because the only way she will get Wolf in bed is if Leah is there, too—as a full participant in the activities.

The other common open relationship rule is "veto power." Wolf and Willow may want to get it on, but Leah has the power to say, "Yes, you may sleep with my husband" *and* "No, you may not sleep with my husband." If you are interested in bedding someone who has a veto-power rule with his or her spouse, it is considered not only polite but also *mandatory* to ask the non-participating partner directly. Don't take your object of lust's word for it. Just. Don't.

If for some reason you can't ask the spouse directly, do not take one step further toward sexual consummation. The community doesn't need the ensuing drama—and neither do you.

Another thing to consider: it's the twenty-first century, and there *still* isn't a cure for AIDS. Even more scary, the number of new cases of HIV and AIDS is actually *rising*, mostly because people, being people, tend to forget things that aren't part of their day-to-day reality. Practice saying these words before you have to say them (and you do have to say them) to any sexual partner with whom you are not in a strictly monogamous relationship: "We are using protection. It's not optional." Practice saying it like you mean it, because you do mean it. Remember, magic can help you find a new (or better) job. It can alter how you perceive the world around you. It can even give you the strength you need to get out of a bad relationship. But it can't cure AIDS.

In general, just remember that sex is an adult activity. It requires adult-level responsible behavior. Go ahead and have a good time. Enjoy! Celebrate the body the Gods gave you in whatever way you and your partner(s) consent to!

Just don't dump your good sense with your pile of hastily discarded clothes, okay?

Getting the Most Out of Your First Pagan Festival

The idea of packing up your ritual finery, camping gear, myrrh beads, altar cloths, tent banners, and organic bug spray and heading out the door to commune with your fellow Pagans in the bosom of Nature for the better part of a week is daunting, to say the least. But everyone should try it at least once—the experience of being completely immersed in Pagan space twenty-four hours a day, even for just a few days, is empowering, thrilling, and a heck of a lot of fun. You may not know anyone when you arrive, but I guarantee if you attend (and speak up at) workshops, take advantage of any offered meal plan, and let people know that this is your first festival, you'll have made a handful of new friends by the time you leave.

I recently spoke with my good friend Andrea Covey about her first Pagan festival experience. Andrea grew up in Oostburg, Wisconsin (population 2,832), and moved to Sheboygan, also in Wisconsin (population 47,782), shortly after she graduated from high school. Andrea had considered herself Pagan for a little less than a year when she and a friend when to Pagan Spirit Gathering (PSG), one of the oldest and largest Pagan gatherings in the country. This is what she had to say about her experience:

BF: How many people were at PSG that year? How did you meet people?

AC: *I think there were about 800 or 900 people attending that year. I'm a social person; I don't have problems talking to strangers. I went to workshops where there were only five or six other people, and we really had a chance to talk about the subject during and after the workshop. There was also a vendor who camped near us and we got to talking. The workshops helped me connect the most, though.*

BF: What was it like, being in all-Pagan space for the first time?

AC: *It was awesome. There were times when I was like, "Oh my God, I don't know a damn thing" because I was new. I felt like a fraud.*

For me, the best part was the women's ritual. We divided ourselves into three groups—not Maiden, Mother, and Crone, but Warrior, Lover, and Wise Woman. We paraded down the main road of camp on our way to the ritual area. Well, I'm not a feminist, but to hear from the people we passed, "Women, we honor you, women we love you" was so empowering. I'd never heard that, and it was very powerful. The men were literally in awe of us. It was the least afraid, most spiritual moment of the week for me. That's when I felt I was in the right space spiritually for me.

BF: What did you bring back with you from that festival?

AC: *There was a workshop on making ritual items out of clay. Most people were making Venus of Willendorfs, but I made a little yin/yang incense burner that I still use. So that's something physical.*

Spiritually, though, I was so new that it was really something to find out that there were other people like me; I wasn't making all this up. I haven't gone back since, mostly because of life, money, a small child, etc., but if I were to go back now, eight years later, I'd get so much more out of it. I definitely want to go back. It cemented my path for me—that wouldn't have happened, or at least happened as soon, if I hadn't gone.

Andrea didn't mention it, but I learned at my first festival that surviving your first Pagan festival with your psyche, your body, your spiritual self, *and* your metabolism intact is a rare event. And I was on staff! I'm now going to tell you some things I wish someone had told me and/or some friends of mine before we novices went out and lived in all-Pagan-all-the-time space for five days.

Remember to Eat and Drink

This is the most important advice I can give you. Many times, the sheer intensity of energy at a Pagan gathering is so sustaining that new attendees forget to eat meals—they simply aren't hungry—and they pay for it later, sometimes with a trip to the nearest emergency room. If the festival offers a meal plan, buy it *and use it*! Even if you're vegetarian, the festival organizers are sensitive to dietary requirements like that. If you're a vegan, ask. They just might be able to help you. At most gatherings, all workshops, rituals, and other activities stop at mealtimes, so you're not going to miss anything by eating. Plus, it's a great chance to sit down and get to know your fellow attendees.

If the festival doesn't offer a meal plan, take some time before you leave to plan and shop for simple, nutritious meals. Attendees who show up on site with a loaf of bread, a jar of peanut butter, a box of raisins, and plans to live off just those items for four or five days are just asking for health trouble. Trust me. I've seen it. Borrow a camp stove if you don't have one and learn how to use it *before* you go! Make sure you have the necessary equipment and supplies to thoroughly wash and sanitize your dishes. A little squirt bottle of bleach is a must. Don't count on there being a picnic table or other eating surface available.

Whether the festival offers a meal plan or not, bring lots of non-caffeinated (caffeine will help dehydrate you) drinks and extra snacks. My favorite Pagan festival treat is a case of bottled pink lemonade. If you can't make or find pink lemonade, buy plain lemonade and a bottle of peppermint extract, and make mint lemonade—it's quite refreshing! I've also found that the strawberry-lemonade flavored Powerade sports drink is pretty tasty. It rehydrates me and there's enough extra "stuff" in it to keep my electrolytes happy. Oh, and stay away from alcohol. You'll probably be high enough on the Pagan energy that you won't need it.

Pack a basic first-aid and outdoor kit

Bug repellent, *sunblock*, Band-Aids, antibiotic cream, and anti-itch cream are essential. Even if the festival is being held on a completely wooded site, you'd be surprised how much sun gets through the leafy canopy. You may get into the spirit of the gathering and decide to wear a bit less clothing (or more revealing clothing) than you usually do. Pack that SPF 1,000 sunblock and *use it*.

A.G. still remembers the time he was at a Pagan festival where there was a small lake on the property. A female attendee went swimming, then accidentally fell asleep face up on the beach for a couple hours—sans sunblock. There were some parts of her that probably had never been exposed to sun, and those bits had second-degree sunburn by the time she woke up. A.G. became aware of the situation when she staggered into the dining-hall area and begged the volunteers cooking dinner (A.G. included) to put aloe lotion on her blistered bits. She hurt so much that everyone was afraid to touch her for fear of causing her more pain. One kind soul eventually smeared aloe on the affected areas, but the consensus among the kitchen volunteers for the rest of the weekend was that the woman had been incredibly stupid not to put on even a little sunblock before dozing off. Don't let this happen to you.

Pack a roll or two of toilet paper; you never know. Remember to take the toilet paper with you on your trips to the bathroom or Porta-John. It does you no good sitting in your tent—I say this from experience, by the way. Also, if you are on any sort of regular medication, even stomach acid pills or over-the-counter allergy tabs, don't forget them! Pack ibuprofen or aspirin. Make sure someone checks you thoroughly for ticks at least once a day or, if you're modest, once you get home.

And don't forget the sunblock!

Don't try to do everything

Just because there are six workshop sessions and two major rituals scheduled per day, it doesn't mean you have to attend each one. After all, now that you've actually come to a festival, you can always come back next year and do everything you missed this year. Give yourself a break once or twice a day (aside from mealtimes) to sit and rest and assimilate what you've learned in the workshops you've already attended. Also, Pagan gatherings are notorious for having a lot (and I mean a *lot*) of quality merchants and craftspeople in attendance. If you're in workshops all the time, when will you be able to go shopping?

If you're not used to attending ritual on a regular (monthly or twice monthly) basis, you may want to limit your ritual at-

tendance to one per day or less. Sweat lodges count as rituals—actually, one sweat lodge should count as two rituals if
you're not used to them. The intense heat and humidity is
very hard on your body. I was on staff at an early Free Spirit
Festival when a young man attended two sweat lodges in one
day and didn't bother to eat at all or drink much before, between, or afterward. He—literally—collapsed, and if the camp
nurse hadn't managed to stuff him full of electrolyte-rich
fluids as fast as she did, we'd have had to call an ambulance.
Sweat lodges can be awesome and deeply spiritually moving,
but they're also exhausting and dehydrating—attend with care.

Get some sleep

It's tempting to stay up until three or four a.m. at the drumming circle and bonfire. If you're determined to do so, save
it for the last night of the festival. Try to get at least 75 to 80
percent of the amount of sleep you normally get at home.
If you're a light sleeper, pack earplugs. With you or without
you, the drumming and fire dancing will go on until almost
dawn—at which time the waking birds get *really* loud. If
there are cabins available, especially cabins with electricity,
try to reserve sleeping space in one. Cabins keep out the rain
and most of the bugs, and if they have electricity, a small fan
may make the difference between being too hot to sleep and
sleeping comfortably. A fan can also act as white noise and
cover most of the drumming and early bird songs. Most cabins offer at least a camp bed, which, if you're over thirty, is a
major improvement to sleeping on the ground.

Ground, ground, and ground again

Before the entire festival experience overwhelms you, find a quiet place, maybe at the foot of a particularly friendly tree, and ground yourself. If you don't know how, or if you're having trouble, find a member of the festival staff to help you. That's what they're there for—to help attendees have a good *and* safe time. If they can't help you, if the person you asked is on his or her way to resolve an overflowing-toilet emergency, they *will* find someone who can help you. If you can't find anyone on staff, grab a workshop presenter. If a person is presenting at a major festival, he or she has enough experience with things Pagan to help someone ground themselves.

Mind your Pagan manners

If a tarot deck, necklace, crystal, drum, or athame is sitting on a merchant's table, it's okay to touch. If any of these items is sitting in someone's campsite or cabin, it's *not* okay to touch. And don't even ask to. Again, if the owner offers to let you touch it, even if he or she is physically *handing* it to you, ask, "May I?" before you even reach for it.

Don't go around saying, "Well, in *my* coven, *we* . . ." Let me be the first to tell you: no one there cares. Don't touch another person's necklace if he or she is wearing it. Period. If you stumble across a couple having sex in the woods, remove yourself from the area immediately. Soap, deodorant, and toothpaste are still your friends. Keep your less-than-flattering comments about other peoples' bodies, tattoos, or ritual or festival garb (or lack thereof) to yourself. Which brings me to . . .

Keep an open mind

A lot of people wear next to nothing—or nothing at all—at a Pagan festival. And I don't just mean in ritual. It's possible you could turn to ask a fellow shopper in the merchant area a question, only to find that he or she is stark naked. If it's a really hot day, the *merchant* may be stark naked. Question: What's the polite thing to do? Answer: Treat them as if they were fully clothed unless invited to do otherwise.

I will never forget my first festival. Early on the first day I met a gentleman who, at that time, was a rather prominent member of a national Druid organization. His festival attire of choice was a neon-green, calf-length cape and knee-high, black-leather biker boots. And that was it. He was also the first uncircumcised male I had ever seen. Considering his outfit, it was kind of hard to miss. A very loud "Oh, my GOD" escaped my mouth before my brain kicked in and said, "That must be what an uncircumcised penis looks like, dummy!" Needless to say, the gentleman always remembered my name every year when we re-met at the same festival . . .

Also, be aware that gay and lesbian couples, as well as men and/or women in three-way (or more) relationships, will likely feel more comfortable expressing affection in public at a Pagan gathering than they do on the streets of your hometown. You may very well see two men or two women holding hands or kissing, or three people of any combination of gender being affectionate right in front of you. If you've never seen it before, it can take a wee bit of getting used to. Be nice and don't say anything.

If there are showers available at the festival site, it's 99 percent probable they're co-ed. I'm just sayin'. If you're the modest type who just cannot wash your girly bits or dangly bits in front of total strangers, plan to shower very late at night or very early (before 6:00) in the morning. If there's a crowd and you have to shower *right now,* close your eyes and face the spray (away from the room) when you get to those sensitive parts. It helps.

Wear a waterproof watch

At my first Pagan gathering, I sweated so much that I shorted out my watch on the second day. Seriously. Ever since then (and that was in 1986), I've only owned waterproof watches. Now I not only don't have to worry about sweating, if I happen to jump into the swimming pool or the pond, I also don't have to worry about my watch fritzing out on me.

Speaking of swimming in ponds, you need to remember to leave Nature alone. Yes, you're in the middle of it. Yes, you worship it. This does *not* mean you should do stupid stuff like staying outside during a major thunderstorm so you can yell at the sky in Old Norse or trying to commune with a snake that's lying across your path. If they tell you water moccasins live on *that* end of the pond, don't go over there! Don't try to make friends with the wasps' nest in the corner of the dining hall. The skunk may be your totem animal. For the sake of your fellow attendees, *leave it alone!*

Oh, and thoroughly clean up your campsite before you leave. Be nice and clean up the one next to you, too.

As you become accustomed to attending Pagan festivals, and get used to the demands put on your psyche and your energy, you can relax *some* of the self-care suggestions: feel free to get a little less sleep and attend a few more workshops.

Take extra-good care of yourself afterward

Aftercare is very important once you get home, to help you recover from the incredible experience and to reintegrate back into your everyday life. In fact, at clothing-optional festivals, aftercare starts on your way out, as there is usually someone posted at the front gate checking to make sure that all exiting participants are wearing some sort of pants and shirt.

In addition to getting used to clothes again, I also strongly recommend that you eat more protein than usual for the next few days (I always make sure I have steak waiting for me in the refrigerator for the first post-festival supper), drink more fluids, and give yourself a chance to catch up on missed sleep. Your body will thank you for the extra attention.

If you can, schedule a day off work after the festival to slowly and gently reintroduce yourself to the non-Pagan world. I realized the importance of this once when I attended a gathering that had "Trash Pirates"—the cleanup crew had an interesting sense of humor and turned their battered truck and regular daily pick-ups of garbage into a major entertainment event. Twice a day, the bandanna-wearing Trash Pirates would come around, huge black skull and crossbones flag fluttering from the makeshift flagpole attached to the truck's cab, singing a horrible song about the joys of being Trash Pirates while one of the crew kept time by banging a stick on the outside of the bed of the truck as they emptied the bagged contents of the fifty-five-gallon trash drums into the back of the truck. The song was truly dreadful, but it kept them and the rest of us amused. It also got stuck in my head and refused to leave; for several days after I got home from this particular festival, I'd sing, "Yar, we be pirates!" every time I threw something in the trash. Fortunately, the song was more or less out of my system before I went back to work.

Don't be surprised if you emotionally fall apart once you get home. For a variety of reasons, I experienced major life-altering events the first three times I attended a Pagan festival. Some were good, some not so good, but all of them were quite a shock to my emotional system. While you're catching up on sleep and stocking up the protein, allow yourself the luxury of a good cry (or two) if you need it.

The most important thing, though, is to have fun. Most of us don't spend all day, every day, in "Pagan space." With a little care and pre-planning on your part, you can have a festival experience wonderful enough and fulfilling enough to last until it's time to go again next year!

I hope that all of these helpful tips will encourage you to go out and experience community. If nothing else, attending a group or community ritual will help you more clearly define your own beliefs and how you do and do not want to express those beliefs. Attending a festival, aside from the awesome opportunity for some serious shopping, can give you a wealth of ideas to incorporate into your own practice.

CHAPTER 3

The Well-Decorated Broom Closet

While it's not overtly Pagan, there is definitely art-work of a Pagan nature in every room of my home. The fireplace mantle is the main family altar. There are statues of gods and goddesses here and there in the house, and lots of original artwork that signi-fies things that are important to us—i.e., water paintings in the west, etc.

—JULIA, EAST STROUDSBURG, PENNSYLVANIA

Whether or not you choose to tell your family, friends, and neighbors that you're Pagan, your home can tell them for you. Artwork, objects, and tchtochkes (Yiddish for "little stuff lying around your house") can all reflect your Pagan-ness as subtly or as overtly as you please.

Subtle Décor

My home contains its share of obvious Pagan art—the huge Green Man poster hanging in the upstairs hallway, the picture of Stonehenge in my daughter's room, and the shrine in the master bedroom are dead giveaways. But there are also some not-so-obvious pieces here and there, like the Brigid's cross hanging over the front door. One of my favorite subtly Pagan touches is my collection of cast-iron kitchen trivets that hang on the dining room wall. To an undiscerning eye, they look like folk art, which they are, but the Pagans will notice the one with brooms in the design (inherited from my nice Methodist grandmother), and smile.

These trivets can be found at flea markets, junk antique stores, and garage sales. I've never actually walked into a store and bought a new one. In fact, my absolute favorite cast-iron trivet is a pentacle—a five-pointed star in a circle that my husband and I found in a filthy, dusty old barn-turned-antique store (our favorite kind!) in Hermann, Missouri. It's had a proud place on my wall ever since we brought it home in 2002.

I have lots of crystals, a year wheel, a green man
and green woman in the kitchen; my apron, which
has a year wheel, and a small shrine to Bastet and
Anubis are by the back door.

—DONNA HAMES, NASHWAUK, MINNESOTA

Another not-obvious thing to do is hang a horseshoe over your front door—points up, of course, so the "good luck" doesn't run out. Hanging a lucky horseshoe over your front door is a time-honored American folk tradition, and no one is likely to think twice about it. You're the only one who needs to know that the crescent shape of the shoe is a religious symbol and that horses have a long, illustrious connection with Paganism—from Epona, the Gaulish horse goddess (who also has a fertility aspect) to the British hobby horse who is part of the mummer's play and morris-dancing tradition and is very much a part of England's May Day celebrations.

If you consider yourself more of a kitchen Witch, then the tools of your art—favorite pots, bread pans, good knives, and so forth—can be openly displayed in your sacred space, i.e. kitchen, and no one will even notice. My German-born mother-in-law lives in Salina, Kansas (population 46,180). She has a flotilla of little "kitchen Witch" dolls (riding on wooden spoons, no less!) hanging from her kitchen ceiling in a *V* formation, and the *V* is aimed directly at the back door. My husband is pretty sure they were placed that way deliberately, to help "sweep" the negativity from her house.

> *Here's another reason why I think people don't hold issue with my choice of faith. My whole home is dedicated in one way or another to nature or Paganism. Right when you enter my home is one of my altars (not my working one, more of a seasonal one on which I do a little work) with a statue of Goddess and God. All my walls are adorned with the many broomsticks I collect and a few of the less standard Witches. I've collected many antique Halloween decorations over the years, and since some were expensive, I proudly display them. A Witch hangs over my dining room table, and I have three in my kitchen. Anyone who didn't know of my faith before gets the idea from even stepping into my home. Too much? Maybe, but I pay for it, so I get to decide what goes on the walls!*
>
> —WITCH OF THE WOODS, MERRIMAC, WISCONSIN

If you prefer to hang pictures on your walls rather than objects, why not start with pictures of your own family? It doesn't matter if you don't have photos of your great-great-grandparents, display what you can. We have a huge collection of family pictures on our dining room wall, going back as far as my grandmother (we have more that go back further, we just ran out of room). We call this our Hall of the Ancestors, and it's often a topic of conversation over supper as we point out various family members to our daughter Rose and tell her stories about each one. Family and ancestors are very important to my husband's spiritual practice, and this is a way for him to express it. Do non-Pagan visitors to our home need to know that? Of course not.

It's hard to find more Pagan art than the work done by the English Pre-Raphaelite artists (ca. 1848–60). The Pre-Raphaelites were inspired by Greek mythology, the Arthurian legends, and many other classic works of literature. Paintings include such figures as Persephone, Medea, the Oracle at Delphi, Circe, Ophelia, and Pandora (there are relatively few males in Pre-Raphaelite art). Some of their paintings even depict scrying, circle casting, and other Pagan activities.

My favorite painting by a Pre-Raphaelite artist is John William Waterhouse's *The Lady of Shalott* (1888), inspired by the poem of the same name by Alfred, Lord Tennyson. The poem is the story of a woman cursed to never leave her tower and join the crowds at Camelot (which she can see in her magic mirror), lest she die. Unfortunately, one day her mirror shows her an image of Lancelot. She immediately falls in love with the handsome knight, leaves her tower, climbs into a waiting boat, and floats to Camelot. Of course she dies before she arrives. The painting is of the critical moment when she chooses to cast off from the dock, sealing her fate. Why do I love it? Well, other than the pure pathos and drama of the moment, and aside from the fact that it is truly a beautiful work of art, I love the message I get from the painting: not even the Gods can save us from our fates. Plus, I think the amount of detail in the painting (the original is approximately eight feet by ten feet; yes, I've seen it) is amazing.

Were the Pre-Raphaelite painters Pagan? Probably not, but one of their "doctrines" was to "study Nature attentively" in order to reproduce it faithfully in their works. They seem to have been embraced by contemporary Pagans for their subjects and themes, yet whenever my nice Episcopalian mother visits, she sleeps under my copy of *The Lady of Shalott* and doesn't even blink.

Why stop at subtly decorating the inside of your home? Various outdoor plants and house decorations can announce your faith to the world—if only the world knew their significance. Before she became too frail to do yard work, my mother-in-law surrounded the outside of her house with plants that have the property to fend off the evil eye, including garlic, datura, and rose bushes. Holly trees and English ivy are both found in pre-Christian symbolism and music. Oak trees feature prominently in ancient and contemporary Pagan lore, and so do rowan, willow, ash, and walnut trees.

My mother-in-law, who swears she is a good Lutheran but is also the most powerful Witch I have ever met, also has at least a dozen small lawn gnomes peeking out from beside her shrubs, next to the lilac bushes, and hanging out with the roses. My husband has already started our collection; as of this writing, four gnomes and one moss-covered rabbit hang out in the shrubbery by the front door, two gnomes live in the dining room, and one guards the perpetual pile of to-do paperwork that lives next to the computer. We also have a huge metal sun/moon face hanging next to the front door. I'm sure our neighbors think we bought it because it's mostly painted the same colors as our house (red and white).

If you use a lot of herbs in your religious observances, either as incense or in various workings, why not grow your own? There is also nothing more spiritually satisfying to a kitchen Witch than growing his or her own vegetables and feeding them to the family. I have the world's blackest possible thumb (which is why I'm not a kitchen Witch), but I've been told by more than one reliable source that this is true—including the source I'm married to.

Obvious Décor

Of course if you want to openly decorate your house with things Pagan, the sky is the limit. Ceramic green-man faces on the wall, pentacle magnets on the refrigerator, and visible shrines in the public area of your house can turn your entire home into sacred space—although subtle artwork can, too.

> *There is no mistaking when you come into my home that we are Pagan! I have plaques of the Lord and Lady, many Native American things, pentacles, etc. everywhere. I don't hide it.*
>
> —JENN, MOUNTAIN HOME, IDAHO

> *Right now, I have all of my Paganish books in a bookcase in my dining room, as well as a phone stand where my Tarot cards live when I'm not using them. I have a large and very colorful astrological wheel cross-stitch displayed on the wall. I put out themed centerpieces on the table for each Sabbat.*
>
> —RAVENNA, DOWAGIAC, MICHIGAN

There are dozens of excellent artists whose work depicts obvious Pagan themes, far too many to mention here, but these are some of my—and my friends'—favorites:

Nybor Mystical Art (www.nyborart.com): Nybor of Haven is well-known on the Pagan gathering and conference circuit and is my personal favorite Pagan artist. It's hard to believe he's colorblind. His work includes faeries, satyrs, goddesses, gods, and a myriad of woodland creatures. I have a print of one of his Crone series hanging upstairs, and plan to acquire more soon!

Susan Seddon Boulet (www.susanseddonboulet.com): Although she passed away in 1997, Susan Seddon Boulet is still a popular artist among American Pagans. Her artwork shows strong Native American influence, but her pictures of goddesses from all over the world are equally distinctive. As of this writing, prints of *Demeter and Persephone* are still available on her website.

Anne Marie Forrester: If you're more interested in taking your Pagan artwork with you in the form of permanent tattoos, check out Anne Marie's site. She has also illustrated some book covers and has a series of greeting cards for each of the Sabbats that are, in a word, awesome. Her website is http://web.mac.com/annemarieforrester.

Alicia Austin (www.aliciaaustin.com): Alicia's work is also strongly influenced by Native American mythology, and even someone who knows next to nothing about Native American myths (that would be me) can tell that this is powerful, divinely inspired stuff. She also seems to have tapped into Russian and Persian folklore for some of her pieces. Definitely worth checking out.

Jen Delyth (www.kelticdesigns.com): Jen is a Welsh artist who is best known for her intricate Celtic artwork. Her annual Celtic Mandalas calendar is an annual purchase in my household; I use it as my family schedule calendar since I usually hang it right next to the refrigerator.

Mickie Mueller (www.mickiemuellerart.com): Mickie is an accomplished artist and illustrator from the Midwest. Goddesses, gods, faerie children, green men, and other magical beings come to life in her paintings. She's even taken some of her favorite works and had them turned into gorgeous, intricate pendants.

Another obvious piece of Pagan décor is a shrine placed where family, friends, and guests can see it. You may not want to be this obvious—not because of the trouble it would cause, but because non-Pagan visitors may become curious and handle your ritual tools and sacred statues. If the thought of someone else handling your altar stuff without asking makes you twitchy, you may want to reconsider being this obvious.

If you have pets, you may want to take their natures and needs into consideration before setting up a permanent shrine. The combination of large, boisterous dogs with strong, wagging tails and a shrine full of breakable objects can only end badly; either the dog will run into the shrine and knock it over or his tail will sweep the surface clean of all your precious statuary. Not that cats are any better. My mother's cat Tye hates it when stuff deigns to clutter a high surface he wants to nap on, and generally makes sure it is bodily removed (by him) before he settles down for an afternoon snooze. I once had a cat who loved to yukk up hairballs on my shrine until I finally got the hint and took it down.

One note about my using the term *shrine* when most people would use *altar*: by my definition, a shrine is any flat surface covered with objects that hold deep personal meaning for you—from pictures of loved ones to a statue of your favorite goddess. A shrine is where you go to sit, meditate, and commune quietly with your God(s). An altar, on the other hand, contains the tools you need for the ritual you are about to perform. The same items can be on both, but an altar is set up for action—i.e., a ritual or magical working—and a shrine is set up for more reflective work.[9] I have not changed my survey respondents' use of the terms to reflect my opinion. What is written in the various responses is what they said.

> We have a small altar set up in our living room that
> consists of a Qwan Yin statue, ancestral urn, dried
> fruits and berries in a dish, and, until it was bro-
> ken, a Buddha statue. We have the "main" altar in

---

9. Also see my article "Is It an Altar or a Shrine?" on *Witchvox.com* (April 19, 2009): http://www.witchvox.com/va/dt_va.html?a=uswi&c=words&id=13188.

our bedroom, and the kids have a small one in each
of their rooms.

—KELTASIA, SHAMOKIN, PENNSYLVANIA

We maintain two shrines/altars in our home—a
healing shrine and an ancestor shrine. We also have
personal altars in other rooms. We have artwork
with Pagan themes: a print of the Oracle of Delphi,
and one of Diana from the Pompeii frescoes, statu-
ary, etc.

—MOONDANCER, WASHINGTON STATE

My survey respondents are not in agreement on if or how to
decorate one's home in a Pagan-y way. Some felt that their
home was part of the "broom closet" and should provide
the same neutral façade as the rest of their lives. Oh, there
were Pagan objects and art pieces in the home, but so subtle
that only another Pagan would notice. Others agreed that
their home was part of the "broom closet" but in a different way—the one place where they could relax and be themselves and be open about who and what they are; their home
décor tended to be much more openly Pagan than the first
group's. Either way, I found some excellent advice and ideas
for my home, and I hope you have, too.

Pentacle dream catchers, statues, books . . . pretty
much anything is visible. I'm very open about my

spirituality, and anybody who visits my home has to be accepting to my ways.

—DEANNA EBERLIN, ADDISON, NEW YORK

I have a banner of flags of the five elements and various Witch curios in my living room. I have crystals all over. I have my bookshelf of Pagan books in my living room also. I keep small Witchy items all over the house. I also have Witches, fairies, and Goddess statues in my yard.

—K, SEVIERVILLE, TENNESSEE

I have Pagan paintings, Goddess statuary, rhythm instruments, singing bowls, and Green Man statuary. I also have a lot of found nature gifts: pine cones, dried pomegranates.

—KIM SCHAUFENBUEL, OWATONNA, MINNESOTA
(POPULATION 24,958)

Decorating for the Holidays

Even if your home décor is not particularly Pagan most of the time, it doesn't mean you can't "go a little wild" during the holidays you share with your Christian neighbors. Just because *you* know that Halloween, Christmas, and Easter borrow heavily from pre-Christian cultural practice, it doesn't mean your fellow small-town residents are aware of the connection. After all, if they're plastering their homes with Witches in October, pentacles (or at least stars) made of lights in December, and pastel bunnies in March and April—don't you think they'll expect you to do the same? Even if they don't decorate for these holidays, they're not likely to care if you choose to.

> *We always have a Yule tree, holly, mistletoe, and a symbolic Yule log. Our big spring thing is Ostara, so Easter gets a pass. Halloween has two faces—the fun side with the dress-up and decorating, and the serious side when my husband and I always go for a Samhain spirit walk when everyone else is in bed. We don't have a problem with the dichotomy—it just works for us.*
>
> —DONNA HAMES, NASHWAUK, MINNESOTA

> *I decorate and celebrate them all, because I don't think it matters why other people celebrate those days but that it is a time when we become more "one" than the rest of the year. It's really a shame that we don't all come together all year around. Of course, when things like Easter come around I don't mind the "commercialization" because I know what Ostara is really about. It is about the rabbit and eggs, so it is okay. Maybe I am weird, but I love the spirit of St. Nick, too. In neither case do I celebrate the Christian aspect, but others don't get it because they too have adopted the Pagan way and*

don't know it! I even hang three ears of corn outside
of my front door starting at Lughnasad.

—JENN, MOUNTAIN HOME, IDAHO

To confirm Jenn's comment, ever since I moved away from the Washington, DC metropolitan area in 2000, I have noticed that people in smaller towns are more likely to decorate their yards and front porches with harvest themes long before the end of October. In my neighborhood, corn stalks, scarecrows, gourds, and hay bales—all of which could be real or fake—were pretty common this past fall. In fact, there were entire stands at the local farmers' market dedicated to selling these harvest decorations. They seemed to be very popular.

Although I am not the type of Pagan to be offended by a nativity scene set up on the courthouse lawn in December, I have to smile when that exact same spot has scarecrows and pumpkins parked on it in September. If my city officials choose to decorate for Mabon on my behalf (even if they have no clue that they're doing so), the least I can do is appreciate their efforts!

Because we have a young child, and just because I like to decorate, my family leaps into the standard holiday decorating frenzy. We carve pumpkins and set out the collection of indoor Witch candle-holders for Halloween. We also have some outdoor decorations, including tombstones, a three-foot-tall skeleton, a "potion shoppe" wall plaque, and a few yard signs with Witches on them. It doesn't matter that I'm proclaiming my "Witchyness" in the front yard for the world to see—it's Halloween, and everyone else on the block is doing the same thing! We just make sure the pumpkins are in and the lights are out by the time we start our Samhain ritual—assuming we even schedule it for the same night as trick-or-treat.

For Yule we always get a tree and a wreath. In this I am blessed to live in a small town—Christmas-tree farms where we can go out and cut down our own tree are easy to get to and reasonably priced. There's something very medieval about choosing and cutting down the tree—which I consider to be a scaled-down version of the Yule log—and dragging it back to the farm owner so we can pay for it. I always try to sing a few very old Yule songs, such as "Please to See the King" or "The Gower Wassail," as we haul the tree back to the car. I think my husband would have preferred less singing and more helping-him-pull-the-tree-through-a-couple-feet-of-snow this past year!

Another way to further Paganize your Yule decorations (as if you need to) is to make them all natural. String popcorn and cranberries to hang on your tree; kids love to do this. When you're done with your tree, you can hang the popcorn/cranberry strands outside in another tree's branches or some bushes, to feed the squirrels and birds that haven't migrated away for the winter. Will your small-town neighbors look at you askance for doing this? Probably not. Be careful, though. Cranberries are tough little fruits, and it's hard to get the needle all the way through them.

Find some pine cones on your next walk through the neighborhood, cover them with peanut butter, roll them in birdseed, and hang them on your Yule tree as well. The squirrels will love them once the holidays are over.

If you think you need an excuse to decorate Ostara eggs and you don't have a kid of your own, borrow someone's for the afternoon. Trust me, the kid will love you for it, even if your kitchen may never fully recover from the extra mess. My daughter is now old enough to remember that at some point in the spring it's time to decorate eggs, and she usually starts begging me to get the food coloring out shortly after Valentine's Day. We usually end up dying two batches—one on Ostara and one at Easter, unless they're very close together. Also, whether it's with your own kid or the one you rented for the occasion, no neighbor is going to look at you strange if you host an Easter egg hunt in your own backyard. Just make sure that some of the plastic eggs have bunny and baby-chick Peeps inside.

As a child growing up in a town of about eight thousand people, I remember my mother bringing in sprigs of pussywillow as soon as the buds were "fuzzy," and putting them in a vase. It was always a sign that spring was finally coming. My mother-in-law not only brings in pussywillow branches, but she also decorates them by hanging small, hand-carved wooden eggs and rabbits on them. She calls this her Easter tree.

Here's what the experts have to say about their decorating habits on the shared holidays of Samhain/Halloween, Yule/Christmas, and Ostara/Easter:

We decorate extensively for Halloween and Christmas with a leaning towards more Pagan-like stuff, but we do put up a small manger scene. In my way of thinking, the manger scene fits in with the stories of the "sun god" being reborn so it doesn't conflict, even though others may think it's Christian only. We do little Easter decorating—mostly with more Pagan features such as colored eggs.

—KELTASIA, SHAMOKIN, PENNSYLVANIA

I don't decorate much, other than a tree for Yule, but I also don't do the modern décor on the tree either. We go out and leave shortbread goods on the trees for the animals and spirits, but the decorations I do put up are for the true Pagan side.

—SPIRITRUNNER, BAKERSFIELD,
CALIFORNIA (PREVIOUSLY IN TAFT, CALIFORNIA)

I still decorate eggs for Easter and put out bright tablecloths and what have you. Halloween is my time. I make costumes like crazy, and I put out all sorts of decorations. Of course, it's less ghosts and goblins and more elegant and spooky-goth. As for Christmas . . . well, we always had a tree and decorations growing up, and the whole season doesn't feel right without lights and all the ornaments I've collected all my life.

—RAVENNA, DOWAGIAC, MICHIGAN

CHAPTER 4

The Discount Superstore Altar

Be creative! The vessel I use to hold water is an old cruet, which was formerly used to mix homemade salad dressing and has a fancy glass stopper. And my altar belonged to a local woman who had used it as a coffee table. The legs fold underneath it like a TV tray. She and her daughter used to play board games on it. It's beautiful, with peacocks inlaid in mother-of-pearl, and I picked it up for twenty-five dollars at her yard sale!

—KELTASIA, SHAMOKIN, PENNSYLVANIA

When I first got the idea for this book I lived in Portales, New Mexico, where the nearest Pagan shop was four-and-a-half hours away in Albuquerque. Although I'd bought, bartered for, or found all my altar items years ago, I looked around my little town and realized that the only option for acquiring new ritual items, other than a small thrift store operated by one of the local evangelical churches, was the Walmart Supercenter located on the north end of town. It was then that I developed my theory: everything I needed to buy for a basic altar—including the altar—I could get at my local, rural Walmart.

Fast-forward five years to a cold, foggy Saturday in February, when my family and I finally put my theory to the test. Chanute, Kansas (population 8,738) is a small town approximately two hours' drive from any major metropolitan area. It has a circa-1930s soda fountain tucked into the corner of the Cardinal Drug Store, where you can still buy shakes, ice cream, and floats, and a railroad-depot-turned-museum that features the life and work of Martin and Osa Johnson, who pioneered the art of filming African wildlife. If there were ever a "Typical Small Town in Kansas" competition, Chanute would probably be in the top five, if not the winner.

I decided that if I could buy everything I need for ritual at the Walmart Supercenter in Chanute, in a town near "the middle of nowhere" and not home to a four-year college or university, chances are good that you can buy everything *you* need for ritual at a discount superstore near you. As it turns out, I was able to prove my theory to be true—with a little input and help from my five-year-old daughter, Rose. Pagan parents take note: little girls who love ritual are natural diviners, and are into princesses, unicorns, and sparkly things make *awesome* assistants if you're shopping for altar and/or ritual items.

I understand that some readers may have some issues with actually shopping at Walmart in light of some recent controversies. You may even have chosen to boycott this particular chain in protest. Everything I bought at Walmart could also be purchased at other discount stores, including Target and Kmart, if you'd prefer. You can get a few of the items I mention in this chapter at Costco and Sam's Club (which is owned by Walmart), but not all, since those superstores tend to focus on bulk and big-ticket items like televisions and trampolines.

However, the controversy and the boycotting does not change the fact that, for many small towns, Walmart may be the only store in town. When I lived in Portales, New Mexico, the Walmart was one of two places in a city of 12,000 that even sold groceries, and it was the only place to buy electronics, magazines, and new baby clothes for thirty miles, and the only place to buy cheap stick incense for ninety miles. Portales is hardly unique; many small-town Pagans face similar non-choices for their shopping needs every day.

That being said, the one item I did not buy at the Walmart Supercenter in Chanute was an altar. Over the years I've bought one bedroom nightstand and one living room end table from Walmart, and either one would do just fine, if possibly be a little crowded, for an altar. In fact, my personal altar *is* the Walmart nightstand, and the drawers are darn useful for storing extra incense, candles, and other altar "stuff." I did price similar nightstands/end tables in Chanute—they cost about sixty dollars, and all had the three most terrifying words in the English language (at least according to my husband) stamped on the boxes: *Some Assembly Required*.

However, I did pick up the following:

Altar Cloth

If one has an altar, one generally covers it with an altar cloth. With Rose's help, I chose a yard of navy-blue cloth with a small silver star pattern embossed on it. This cloth would be perfectly appropriate for any moon-phase ritual. The Walmart fabric/craft section also always has a nice selection of seasonal fabric that would work for Sabbat altar cloths; if you'd rather have a moon motif on your Esbat altar covering, wait for Halloween and pick some up then. I usually lay an old bath towel down on my altar to go under the altar cloth on the theory that if something spills or a candle drips, the towel will absorb it, and the towel will fit in the washing machine while the altar won't. I didn't buy a bath towel at Walmart, figuring that everyone (not just me) has plenty of not-quite-good-enough-for-company towels in their house already that could be used for this purpose. At our home, we call them "dog towels," since their primary function is to dry the dogs on bath day.

Candlesticks and Candles

I found candlesticks in the housewares section that would work on my altar. They're clear glass, somewhat heavy (which translates into "hard to knock over"), and in a nice classic/Colonial style. I bought three—one for the God candle, one for the Goddess candle, and one for the maiden/self/ancestor (depending on your tradition) candle in between the two. Rose has a habit of sniffing various scented candles every chance she gets—she learned it from me—but together we picked out two Williamsburg gray/blue taper candles for the God and Goddess and a cream one for the center candle. We decided they'd look nice with the blue altar cloth.

Athame

There were two choices at the Chanute Walmart Supercenter for athames: the housewares section and the outdoor/camping section, and neither one had the traditional double-edged dagger blade. Kitchen Witches or those following deities with a caretaking or domestic aspect would probably be very happy with some of the nicer black-handled chopping knives from the housewares section. Since I honestly don't enjoy cooking and, more importantly, because my patron deity is Herne, Lord of the Hunt, I headed for the outdoors and camping section of the store. The very nice sales clerk didn't even blink at the sight of a chunky middle-aged woman (i.e., obviously not a hunter) with a small child being very decisive about hunting knives, and pretty soon a wooden-handled Buck knife with a four-inch stainless steel blade and a handy black sheath was resting in the bottom of my shopping cart.

Chalice and Wine

Since the ritual wine (or juice) is to be shared among all present, I wanted a good-sized chalice, and the housewares section didn't disappoint me. I found two-to-a-box white-wine glasses. Yes, they're clear glass, but they match the candlesticks, and I have a spare in case the first chalice breaks.

Some Walmarts have liquor sections, but since Kansas has separate liquor stores, there wasn't one at the Walmart Supercenter in Chanute. I did, however, find some POM Wonderful® brand 100 percent pomegranate juice, perfect for Ostara or, with the dark red color, a full-moon ritual. Please note, though: my husband A.G. said the pomegranate juice was awfully sour.

Pentacle

This is the tool that is going to take a little creative effort if you're determined to get everything you need at a discount superstore. I found a plain wooden disk six inches in diameter in the craft section. A little digging in the desk drawer at home unearthed an old plastic protractor to help me place the five points. I borrowed one of Rose's black markers, and in about five minutes I had a perfectly drawn pentacle (or as perfectly drawn as I will ever get). You could also use watercolor or craft paint to decorate your pentacle, and those are both available at Walmart. Pagan parents: buy extras and let your kids draw and decorate their own. The wooden disks are only about a dollar apiece.

Incense

Although I prefer loose incense burning on a charcoal, Walmart doesn't stock frankincense, myrrh, and copal, much less the packs of special round incense charcoals with the little indentation at the top. So I had to settle for a decent-looking soapstone stick incense burner and some stick incense I found near the housewares section. I'm awfully picky about my stick incense, but I thought the "Warm Spices" flavor wouldn't be too bad, especially since you get three scents in the same package—vanilla, apple pie, and cinnamon. After some experimentation, I've discovered that, once lit, the vanilla smells like burning soap, the apple pie smells like cheap aftershave, but the cinnamon isn't too bad. It doesn't smell much like what it's supposed to, but on the other hand, the smell doesn't make me gag. I may keep trying the Walmart scents to see if there's one I like.

Salt and Water

In the same section with the incense, incense burner, and potpourri, I found a faux ceramic clam shell that is the perfect water vessel for my altar. In the candles section, I found a shallow, clear-glass votive holder that looks like it was made to hold salt. I sent my husband on a quest to the food aisles, and he came back with a box of sea salt. Perfect!

Cakes

I have an abundance of appropriate plates in my kitchen to hold cookies for Cakes and Wine, and bowls that make functional libation bowls, so I didn't buy any. I did, however, pick up a package of Pepperidge Farm Verona cookies (the round ones with the strawberry or apricot jam in the center; I chose strawberry), just to prove I could, because their shape makes them perfect for full moon rituals and, ultimately, because they made a great snack on the long car ride home. For the photo in this chapter, I picked up a package of molasses cookies.

Of course, you can always buy the ingredients to make your own cookies at any Walmart that sells groceries. But if you do, go with a popular recipe like chocolate chip or oatmeal raisin. Some friends of ours once offered to make cakes for a ritual. They used a "traditional Witchcraft" recipe for ritual cakes that were dry as dust and had no sweetening whatsoever. Sometimes traditional does not mean tasty; I can't imagine offering the Gods a libation I'm not willing to eat or drink myself, can you?

So what's left? What wasn't I able to purchase at the Chanute Walmart Supercenter that I needed to complete my altar? A wand, for one thing, and an image of the God and Goddess. On a walk around my block I found some tiny acorns and sweet gum-tree seed pods—each of which would make a perfect God image for my altar. A pine cone would work, too. For the Goddess image, I snipped a long piece of English ivy that grows all over my front porch and twisted it into a small wreath, which I placed around the base of the Goddess candle. As I write this, it's almost March in Kansas; naturally growing flowers (my first choice) are in short supply right now. Besides, in English folklore, ivy is a symbol of divine femininity. If you want a more permanent Goddess image, Walmart—and Hobby Lobby—sells sea shells, and I was able to pick up a nice cowrie shell at my local Hobby Lobby for not very much money.

I found a working wand in my front yard after an ice storm downed some red maple tree branches. I chose one that was the right length, peeled the bark off, and sanded the ends. I may eventually decorate it with other items I find in my neighborhood as I walk my dog this spring, like bird feathers. You could also pick up a wooden dowel in the craft or hardware section at Walmart, cut it to the length you want, and decorate it any way you like.

No, the Walmart pieces don't exactly fit my altar décor taste, which runs toward rustic, homemade, and folk art; nor are they reflective of my chosen deities in style or color— with the exception of the Buck hunting knife. That being said, I would not be ashamed to perform ritual with them, and at some point I probably will use at least some of what I bought that day in circle (with the possible exception of the incense).

The Walmart altar, ready for ritual. Doesn't it look nice?

Oh, and my final bill for the day? Without the altar and with a thirty-dollar Buck hunting knife, I spent just about one hundred dollars—cookies, salt, and POM juice included.

Other Shopping Opportunities

If you just can't bring yourself to shop for ritual and altar items at Walmart, don't panic! Check out garage sales, flea markets, junky little antique stores, and estate sales. Go on an altar-piece expedition at the nearest Goodwill or other thrift store. With a little time, effort, and patience, you're very likely to find exactly what you want for next to nothing—like my prized pentacle cast-iron-pot trivet that set me back a whole three bucks at a junky antique store in Hermann, Missouri.

If your town has a paint-your-own ceramic shop, you are in luck. For just a few dollars and an evening or two of sanding, painting, and gossip with the other patrons, you can have a custom chalice, cake plate, salt dish, candlesticks, and water bowl.

A ritual tool is not made more powerful by a high price tag or fancy decoration, but by use, by respect, and by intent. Let me give you an example: when I found myself unexpectedly living alone a few years ago, I went to the local flea market to pick up some kitchen items. I was broke, but I needed pots to cook in. One of my finds was an old white enamel pasta pot, for next to nothing. It came with a few dings in the enamel, but I have proudly served my coven many a soup, stew, or lasagna whose noodles were cooked in that pot. That pot is practically part of my tradition now. I wouldn't trade it for anything.

Also, don't be afraid to scour the curio shelves, kitchen cabinets, attic, and china cabinet in your own house; you may already have every altar piece you need for free!

Shopping Online

There are also more places to buy Pagan supplies online—so many, in fact, that I could probably fill a whole chapter, if not a whole book, describing every one. Here are the ones my survey respondents recommended:

AzureGreen (www.azuregreen.com): If Witchvox (witchvox .com) is the flagship website for Pagan networking and information, AzureGreen is the Witchvox of Pagan shopping sites. The prices seem reasonably decent, and the selection is excellent—there's something here for all pantheons and paths—Celtic, Norse, Egyptian, Buddhist, Roman, Greek, Hindu, and more.

CafePress (www.cafepress.com): Pagan artwork, sayings, and symbolism on T-shirts, mugs, bumper stickers, hoodies, mousepads, baby onesies, and pretty much anything you can think of. Slightly pricey, and the shirt sizes never seem to go above 3X, but you can't beat the selection.

Mountain Rose Herbs (www.mountainroseherbs.com): If I did not live near a natural food co-op, I would be a regular customer. In addition to more herbs, teas, and spices than I've even heard of, this site features all-natural soaps, shampoos, aromatherapy oils—and bottles, jars, cloths, bags, wax, etc. for the kitchen Witch who wants to assemble his or her own. This site was mentioned frequently by the survey respondents.

Abaxion (www.abaxion.com): This site features mostly silver jewelry with something for pretty much any Pagan's tastes. The prices seem reasonable.

eBay (www.ebay.com): If you love virtual flea markets and the thrill of bidding on a much-coveted item, you probably already know that eBay was designed just for you. There are some bargains, but typing *Pagan* into the search box yielded some really odd stuff—like the "Pagan Wiccan! Healing incense sticks!" or the haunted skull ring I saw recently. Avoid the hype, know what you can afford, and have fun.

Etsy (www.etsy.com): If handmade items are more to your liking, check out this site. There are lots of listings for soaps, lotions, and blended oils when you do a search on *Pagan*. Not everything on the site is made by hand, but a lot is—and if you buy it, you're supporting a Pagan artisan.

13moons.com (www.13moons.com): This is a classic Pagan supply site, easy to navigate and not overly pricey. A very nice selection of items.

The Blessed Bee (www.theblessedbee.com): Pagan supplies, a humor page, a recommended-book list—I could spend all afternoon on this site. Again, the prices seem to be comparable to the other sites. My favorite from the humor page: "I love nature as much as anyone. I just don't want to become bear poop."

Don't Overload on Stuff

Just because there is a lot of cool Pagan stuff out there doesn't mean you need all of it. And there's nothing like packing up to move a thousand miles to make a person realize just how much "Pagan stuff" you have. I began to ponder this as I was packing for our most recent move last year,[10] and recently revisited the subject for this chapter.

What are the basics of Pagan practice? What do we really need in order to connect with our God(s) in a mutually satisfactory manner? I'll get to what I think we need in a minute.

---

10. This was either while packing up my third box of ritual supplies or my eleventh box of Pagan books. I can't remember.

In the meantime, here's a whole list of what we don't need—but we think we need—in order to be happy, active Pagans.

Jewelry

I used to be so very guilty of this one. At one point (about thirteen years ago), I wore at least one ring on every finger—including thumbs—and four separate pendants twenty-four hours a day / seven days a week, including while sleeping and in the shower. My ears are double-pierced, and only my normal aversion to pain prevents me from acquiring even more holes than that. It's a wonder I didn't drown in the bathtub from the extra weight of all that silver! And whenever I was in ritual, it was even worse: I'd add at least three (sometimes four!) more necklaces, two wrist bracelets, and two ankle bracelets. Did all this bling make me a better priestess? Of course not. There's an old joke in the Pagan community, and like most jokes it has a seed of truth in it: Have you heard of the High Priestess hundred-yard dash? Any priestess who even makes it to the finish line wins!

Even Magrat Garlick, the young Witch in Terry Pratchett's *Discworld* novels, eventually figures out that jewelry does not improve her spiritual practice.

Ritual objects

We may be spiritual beings, but we are not immune to the fallacy of "keeping up with the Joneses." Pagan tchtochkes and other items wax and wane in and out of fashion. A few years ago, everyone in my local community who thought they were cool (and had seventy bucks they didn't need) bought wands that were made from tree branches that had grown in a spiral pattern because of wild grapevines or other vines that had twined around them. They were pretty, and I admit I seriously wanted one, but I wonder how many of those wands are still in use today.

After jewelry, my money pit was, and is, tarot decks. Back in the mid-to-late 1980s, when the publication of a new themed deck was a much bigger, more rare event than it is today, I bought the Mythic Tarot—not because I was (nor am I now) even remotely drawn to working with the Greek pantheon, but because everyone I respected and admired and who, for the most part did have Greek patron deities, bought the Mythic Tarot. I never used it, and eventually gave it away along with ropes of myrrh-bead necklaces, a Daughters of the Moon tarot deck (basically unused), a baby dragon oil lamp, a couple of old video cabinets (i.e., altars), and a veritable forest of candlesticks—all purchased because they were "in" or "trendy" at the time—and, for the most part, never used.

Speaking of altars

They're nice, they're convenient, but they're not always necessary. My husband, for instance, feels mostly spiritually connected when he's working in his vegetable garden and then cooking the results of that garden for his family. His altars, then, are the dirt in the garden and the stove and countertops in the kitchen, as I suspect they are for many kitchen Witches. I'm not saying altars aren't good and useful for ritual; if nothing else, they keep burning candles and sharp implements off the floor, but how fancy does your altar—the actual piece of furniture—need to be? And if you have more than one, ask yourself: how many of the deities honored by their own altar in your home could be better served by you acting as their hands and doing their work in the world?

Now I'm not saying we need to get rid of everything—jewelry, altars, candlesticks, statues, etc., and rely solely on energy, visualization, and our own good deeds to express our spirituality. Pagan practice is undoubtedly enriched beyond measure by these supplemental symbols. But it is easy for too much "stuff" to overwhelm and clutter up the fundamental simplicity of our call to serve our Gods as best we can. If I have more ritual robes hanging in my closet than I do everyday clothes, something is definitely wrong with my priorities. After all, unlike jewelry, I can only wear one robe at a time, and—according to some people—we're supposed to be skyclad (naked) in ritual anyway.[11] I have a weakness for books, but I do my research, evaluate the authors whose words resonate with me the most, and limit the number of books I buy in order to avoid redundancy. (I do this with both Pagan and dog-training books, by the way.)

Serving the Gods, doing their work here on Earth, and giving each other a helping hand as best we can—that's back to the basics of Pagan practice, no matter how many props we buy.

I still wear too much jewelry, though!

---

11. Not that I necessarily agree, but some Pagans think so.

CHAPTER 5

Minimum Daily Requirements

I do feasts for each of the seasonal celebrations; I give offerings on the moons of each month. I give honor to my Gods daily. It's really hard to say what all I do because it's so ingrained into my daily life.
—DEANNA EBERLIN, ADDISON, NEW YORK

Minimum Daily Requirement—the phrase the United States government uses to determine the least amount of any given vitamin, mineral, or other nutrient you need every twenty-four hours in order to achieve and maintain optimum health. But what is the minimum daily requirement for Pagan spiritual practice? What do you need to do every day in order to achieve and maintain a relationship with your God(s)?

For some of us—Emigrants, mostly—our spiritual minimum daily (or at least weekly) requirements include contact with other Pagans. I am a perfect example of this. In 1985, when I first realized I was Pagan, I lived about twenty-five miles north of Baltimore, in Bel Air, Maryland. My first husband, a nice guy but unable to see much beyond his born-again Christian background, was understandably not happy about my studies. While originally he didn't discourage me from attending Pagan events in Baltimore and Washington, DC, he didn't exactly encourage me either.

As time went on, though, he became increasingly hostile to my religious studies and activities, and eventually filed for divorce. Consequently, the only time I felt like a "real Pagan" was when I was away from my own home and in the presence of my fellow coveners and community members. As a result, I filled my life with as many away-from-home spiritually oriented events as I could: I helped start (and run) Free Spirit Gathering, one of the biggest Pagan gatherings on the East Coast; I held office in the local community organization that oversaw the gathering; I was a Saturday afternoon regular at the local Pagan bookstore; I volunteered to write for and help do layout on the quarterly community newsletter; and I attended as many open rituals and classes as I could. Between classes, gatherings, planning meetings, rituals, quarterly community business meetings, newsletter work, and hanging out at the bookstore, I wasn't home much. But I got my minimum daily requirement of Pagan-ness.

I still struggle with this; twenty-five years later (as of this writing), I'm still not very good at being Pagan by myself. Much as it pains me to admit this publicly, I have yet to be able to start even a daily observance beyond my pre-sleep prayers and stick with it longer than a few days. I'm a former Girl Scout—I love Nature as much as the next person if not more. Yet a concert of Pagan musicians and/or singers is far more likely to feed my soul than a solo hike in the woods with my dog. I'm also far more likely to celebrate the Sabbats or observe moon cycles when there are other people in my life to celebrate with. If it's "just us"—i.e., my family—I may not observe the holiday or full moon at all. It's very similar to the fun of preparing, say, Thanksgiving dinner when family and friends are coming over versus cooking that much food on an ordinary day for just one person. For me, the incentive just isn't there.

I suspect that many Emigrants have the same problem when they move to a small town. Contact with others is easy in a large city with its open community events and Pagan shops that serve as information, gossip, and social hubs, but nearly impossible in a small town where the nearest organized Pagans (at least as organized as Pagans ever get!) could be several hours' drive away.

A recent glance at the Kansas and Missouri events pages on Witchvox.com confirms this. Pagans who live in or near

Kansas City have a plethora of weekly, monthly, and annual community activities to choose from, including drumming circles, public rituals, workshops, meetups, Pagan choir practice, study groups, at least two large shops, a major festival every Memorial Day weekend, and several minor gatherings spread throughout the year. There is a working public transit system for those who have no car, so getting to these events—even the festival, if you hire a taxi—is possible. Not cheap, but possible. If you are spiritually "charged" by being in the presence of your fellow Pagans, Kansas City, Kansas/Missouri, is a good place to be. If, on the other hand, you live a couple hundred miles due west, in Salina, Kansas, you have far fewer options. There is a shop about sixty-five miles away in Hutchinson that also hosts open circles, but that's about it. If you don't have access to a car, you can't get to the nearest Pagan activities. It's not physically possible.

For an Emigrant who is used to a fair amount of regular contact with fellow Pagans, actually doing what is necessary to maintain one's spiritual minimum daily requirement is tough. On the other hand, even in a small town it's possible to find like-minded individuals and arrange to meet with them on a regular basis.[12] Several Hometowners reported that they also find a way to celebrate daily, monthly, or even just on the Sabbats with their non-Pagan family and friends.

---

12. For further discussion on creating Pagan community in your small town, see chapter 7.

I spend time with the Goddess on a regular basis. I walk in my yard and admire Her handiwork all around me.

If my family and I are together on a Sabbat, I will prepare a special dinner to fit the holiday, give an explanation and a blessing, and share the meal with my family. They are quite receptive as long as I don't go overboard.

—K, SEVIERVILLE, TENNESSEE

I try to be active on a spiritual level daily, even if it's just chatting with like-minded individuals on the Internet. Basically I practice alone but do attend cybercircles.[13]

—KELTASIA, SHAMOKIN, PENNSYLVANIA

I attend Sabbats, read, meditate, and write music and poetry.

—FERGUS, MONONA, WISCONSIN (POPULATION 8,532)

I do as much as possible to protect and appreciate the earth.

—DARREN, OWATONNA, MINNESOTA

I talk with my deities every day, celebrate full and dark moons, and honor the changing seasons and the great festivals. Sometimes alone, sometimes with my husband, friends, daughter-in-law, or granddaughter.

---

13. Chapter 6 will cover the Internet aspects of Paganism in more depth.

Sometimes to honor Hecate I just take my dog for a late walk.

—DONNA HAMES, NASHWAUK, MINNESOTA

Donna makes a good point: there are ways to honor the Gods and practice our spirituality that have nothing to do with formal ritual or other people. My family shares our lives with three dogs—two of whom are definitely representatives of family/ancestral deities we feel a deep connection with. The third has her own relationship with Hecate. If I choose to, I can (and do) consider caring for the dogs (feeding, walking, training, grooming, cuddling, taking them to the dog park or the pet supply store, playing fetch, etc.) as service to their Gods and, therefore, active daily spiritual practice. For someone as extroverted and community-oriented as myself, I see this as a step in the right direction toward a more private, personal practice.

My husband, on the other hand, is definitely an introvert. He would probably be deliriously happy if he never attended another public Pagan event again. He is gracious and polite whenever I manage to drag him to various Pagan Pride celebrations, weekend gatherings, and open rituals, but they're not really his thing. On the other hand, my spouse finds his deepest spiritual connection in the garden; he loves to organically grow heirloom fruits and vegetables and is never happier than when he's spent a warm weekend afternoon with his hands in the dirt. He's already teaching our daughter the spiritual aspects of gardening; she's an apt pupil and will work in the garden with her father for hours at a time. It also feeds his soul to take those homegrown fruits and vegetables and make fantastic meals for his family. Spiritrunner seems to feel the same way:

> *I'm very much a kitchen Witch, so I do my craft every day with meals and drink. I thank the Goddess for the day I've had (good or bad), because I know it could always be worse—or non-existent at all.*

It's hard to have a garden in the middle of the city, but—as anyone who regularly listens to the National Public Radio program *A Prairie Home Companion* (specifically, "The News From Lake Wobegon" section) can attest—growing tomatoes is not only a common hobby in a small town, it's practically a requirement!

A.G. is not the only one who prefers a less "crowded" spiritual practice. Other survey respondents also had great ideas about how to express their spirituality daily, weekly— even monthly—without help from anyone else:

> *Daily devotionals on my balcony, and I'll be doing a fire in my pit today in the backyard. I'm usually pretty quiet. I'm solitary, so most of my work is done in my home or on my property.*
>
> —WITCH OF THE WOODS, MERRIMAC, WISCONSIN

> *I try to remain mindful of how I interact with nature and take steps to minimize my negative impact. I also try to live more according to the seasons,*

changing my diet and activities to coincide with the
passing of time.

—BECCA, CLOVIS, NEW MEXICO

Book Basics

I can't remember the source, but I saw an article once that said American Pagans tend to read much more than the average citizen. After seeing the answers to the survey I sent out to collect input for this book, I have to agree. Over and over again, the survey respondents said that a big part of their daily spiritual practice is reading. In a big city or a small town, alone on the couch after supper or as part of a Pagan book discussion group, this is one activity all Pagans everywhere can share.

Even though pretty much every Pagan tome ever written—fiction and non-fiction—is available via the Internet with a credit card and just a couple clicks of the mouse, many of us like to save money—and trees—and try to get books from the library, myself included. But some towns are so small there is no library. One survey respondent even said that her town's library shared space with the local tanning salon!

Sadly, the majority of the survey respondents expressed concern that any good Pagan book in their library wasn't there for very long. Whether the books disappeared because the thief was afraid to expose his or her interest in Paganism and publicly check the book out of the library or whether the thief was trying to prevent anyone from reading such "evil" material, I cannot say. I suspect, though, that the Pagan-positive books disappear pretty much equally for both reasons. And, as Spiritrunner points out, the books that are left aren't all that good:

> *In Taft, the only books in the "Pagan" section insinuated that we're all devil-worshipers.*

On the other hand, some small-town libraries have some pretty darn good books on the shelves. Manitowoc, Wisconsin (population 32,764), may have a public transportation system that is limited to within the city limits, but it has a decent selection of Pagan books for beginners—and they're even on the shelves, ready to be checked out.

> *The public library in our town has a number of books on comparative religions, Goddess worship, crystals, astrology, and palm reading—nothing like Margot Adler or Starhawk, but they do have Ronald Hutton's books, so there is enough there to give someone a start and help them find more detailed reading.*
>
> —DONNA HAMES, NASHWAUK, MINNESOTA

If you can't find books that are specifically about Paganism in America (or anywhere else) at the beginning of the twenty-first century on the shelves, don't give up on your local library just yet. It very likely has plenty of information on the following subjects that might prove useful to the Emigrant's *and* the Hometowner's connection to Deity:

Sustainability

Growing and preserving more of your own food isn't just a way to save money; it's also a great way to express your spirituality. Julia from East Stroudsburg teaches it to her group as part of her regular practice:

> *Daily devotions and work with my gods, monthly full moons, and a monthly drumming circle—where we also teach sustainability arts like canning, woodworking, gardening and the like.*

If you live in a small town, it's likely you'll have room for at least a small vegetable or herb garden. If you've recently moved to a small town and have always wanted to grow at least some of your own food, now is a good time to learn how. Organic gardening is safer for the earth and everyone on it—do you know how to compost and how to organically deter bugs and other pests (deer, rabbits, your dog, raccoons, etc.) from eating your produce? Once you've organically grown some fruits or vegetables, do you know how to can them or otherwise safely preserve them for the winter months? A.G. and I thought we did, but we never checked to see if basic canning instructions and boiling times changed if you lived above a certain altitude. As a result, we had a scary, beer-smelling epidemic of Foaming Exploding Jars of Tomatoes in our pantry for a week when we lived in Portales, New Mexico, which is roughly four thousand feet above sea level. Most libraries have an extensive gardening and food preservation section.

Also, since "going green" is so popular, libraries are stocking books on how to live more gently on the earth—and use fewer natural resources—for every age group. Find one in the children's section and teach your kids how to help save the planet. Get one for yourself and read up on how to be "green" and save on your utility bills at the same time.

Cooking

Spiritrunner, from Bakersfield, California, talked earlier about cooking for others at Sabbats and Esbats, and my husband A.G. considers the act of preparing his contribution to the post-holiday feast to be part of the ritual itself. Whether you're truly a kitchen Witch or just aspire to be not so inept around large heat-producing appliances and cauldrons (i.e., saucepans) full of bubbling, er, stuff, this is a great way to expand your knowledge and repertoire. The library probably also has just the cookbook you need to help you re-create your great-grandmother's candied walnut recipe when you want to honor and remember her at Samhain.

If your deities and primary spiritual inspiration come from a specific culture—Greek, Roman (Italian), Irish, Middle Eastern—and you weren't raised by or around immigrants from that culture, chances are your library will have a cookbook on the shelves that covers the basics of the cuisine.

The book(s) may even include holiday décor and customs as well.

For example, my mother-in-law grew up in rural Germany and has passed many of the family recipes down to her son. Fortunately for me (but not for my waistline), my husband loves to cook traditional German food for his family, and he's always looking for more hearty German recipes to add to his repertoire. He's also heard a lot of stories from his mother about how holidays, Christmas and Easter mostly, were celebrated when she was a child. Unfortunately, she's forgotten a lot of the decorating details (being a preteen in Germany during World War II can really mess with your childhood memories) and, in some cases, how to make a specific holiday cookie or bread, but a few "homemade" spiral-bound and stapled German cookbooks we found at various Oktoberfests and street fairs have helped fill in some of the gaps.

Cookbooks can also help you with spellwork. As you cook more and more, you become more adept at following a recipe and then adjusting the recipe to fit your personal tastes. You can transfer your recipe-following and recipe-modification skills to creating workings that accomplish pretty much what you need them to. You may even find that cooking becomes a whole new way for you to eat well and perform spells at the same time.

A good basic cookbook from the library can also come in handy if you're not particularly adept in the kitchen (that would be me) and have been invited to a private group or public ritual. In twenty-five-plus years in the Pagan community, I have attended very few rituals that didn't include a lavish potluck meal beforehand, during, or afterwards. Unfortunately, most people who either didn't grow up with the church-potluck tradition or haven't attended even a few public or private group rituals don't know the unspoken rule about the food aspect of these events, so I'm going to step up and tell you: it's tacky to bring store-bought or store-made food as your contribution to a pre- or post-ritual potluck. I'll even tell you the rest of the unspoken rule—the exceptions to the first part of the rule: a famous red-and-white-striped bucket of fried chicken, brownies, or cupcakes from a box mix (with store-bought frosting on the cupcakes, of course), or a gallon or two of ice cream in a cooler at a summer ritual.

Why are these the exceptions? There are never enough meat dishes at community potlucks; brownies are chocolate, and chocolate in any form is always welcome; cupcakes are fun no matter how old you are; and ice cream—well, pretty much everyone likes ice cream. And if you bring some cones, paper bowls, and/or an assortment of toppings—sprinkles, chocolate (remember, chocolate is always welcome), or butterscotch sauce—your potluck contribution will be even more enthusiastically received.

The point is, with help from a cookbook from the library, you can make a nice potluck dish for not much more than you'd spend on a large container of that nasty store-bought potato salad. With a little inspiration from a basic cookbook, you can develop your own specialty dishes for each holiday, whether it's bread for Lammas, apple pie for Mabon, or plain old-fashioned chocolate fudge for Yule. My specialty? Divinity fudge (egg whites, Karo syrup, sugar, and vanilla)—it's easier to make than you think. It has to be, if I'm cooking it!

Buddhism

Buddhism is often welcome where Paganism is not. I'm not advocating that you give up your Pagan practice and join a Buddhist monastery (or convent), but a library book that covers the basics of Buddhist meditation could greatly enhance your daily practice. A book on simple yoga stretches and poses could be equally valuable, especially if sitting still to meditate really isn't your thing. I tend to incorporate some Buddhist breathing practices into my nightly prayers because I enjoy them; they speak to me.

Also, if I'm actually being pressed about my religion and it's a situation where I don't feel safe coming out of the broom closet (like at work or my husband's work), I can say—and have said—with perfect honesty that I am a really lousy Buddhist. Most people have a basic mental image of Buddhists as peaceful, relatively harmless people, and it saves me from having to face the possible negative backlash of telling someone I'm a Witch. Plus, since most Buddhists are vegetarians and anyone who has seen me eat—a group that could include my or my husband's co-workers—knows that I am pretty close to carnivorehood (I had to sneak fried chicken into the one Buddhist retreat I attended so I wouldn't starve to death!), my announcement that I am a Buddhist usually sparks some interesting discussion about my dietary practices, and any thoughts the querent has about anything else I may be into that's "a little weird" usually disappear as I rhapsodize about my husband's grilled lamb recipe.

Does the querent need to know that I'm a Witch who incorporates Buddhist discipline to quiet and train my mind and breathe rhythmically during guided meditation? Of course not!

History

In the Don't Let This Happen to You category, a Pagan professor friend told me this story: While teaching an American history class, he once gave a pop quiz on the previous lecture about the Salem witch trials. In answer to the question, "What side of town did most of the people accused of being witches come from and why?" one clever student answered, "The east, because that's where all the witch stores were." (Correct answer: The east, because the rich people tended to live on the east side of town and were also the majority of the accused, according to the book *Salem Possessed* by Paul Boyer and Stephen Nissenbaum.) Other students were quite adamant in their quiz answers that Tituba (the slave who taught the little girls some basic divination and love charms) was, in fact, a solar goddess worshipped by the local Native American tribe.

We had a good laugh at his students' expense, which could happen to you if you were to accidentally espouse similar misinformation at a public Pagan event (or in an on-line forum). A basic understanding of American history, not only the Salem witch trials but also the process our Founding

Fathers went through to ensure our right to worship as we choose, can only make us better spiritual practitioners.

Many established covens that train and initiate their students also require that their students have a basic working grasp of the history of Western civilization. This is especially important if your God or Gods come from the Greek, Roman, or Celtic pantheons. You will have a much deeper appreciation of your God and/or Goddess if you know something about the culture He or She came from and the history of that culture. If the idea of a thick history text seems a bit daunting, start in the children's book section of the library; you will often find factually sound yet easy-to-digest history books there.

Science

Second only to history as non-Pagan required reading in some covens are books on basic science: physics, chemistry, and biology. The premise is you will have a better appreciation of the mysteries of life and the cosmos if you understand a little bit about how they work. Imagine how much more you would appreciate the unique nature and properties of the various stones and crystals you use if you knew a little bit about basic geology, or how much better astrology would work for you if you read up on astronomy.

I will be the first to admit that I am probably the most scientifically challenged person you will ever meet, partly because of a particularly useless independent-study junior high science program and partly because I'm just not all that interested. I have reduced grown men to literal tears of frustration because I simply cannot grasp how a simple cassette tape records and replays sound even after they tried to explain it to me for the better part of an hour (and please don't try if you ever meet me at a festival or workshop weekend—I guarantee I still won't understand). My husband, who started his college career as a microbiology major, has given up trying to explain anything even remotely scientific to me. Now when I ask him how or why something is, he'll answer, "It's magic." Frankly, this answer is usually good enough for me!

That being said, I took a Physics of Music class when I needed another science elective in college. Being a hobby musician, I thought it'd at least be relevant. Turns out it was also relevant to my Pagan practice. The idea that every single atom in the Universe vibrates (and consequently produces a note of music) expanded my worship of the Divine in some pretty profound ways. Look for books on string theory in your local library. I'll bet you can find at least one.

Another entry in the Don't Let This Happen to You category: My Pagan professor friend shared another story with me about the time he was lecturing on ancient Chinese history in a world civilization course. One student actually raised her hand and asked, "Why didn't the Chinese use their dragons to scare off the invaders?" Yes, she was serious. Apparently she had recently seen a television show that was a "mockumentary" about the evolution of dragons (I actually saw the show—I was impressed as heck by the computer graphics) and didn't realize it was a fake. My five-year-old may not be a science whiz, but she is in a hardcore dinosaur phase. Rose has several books on her bookshelves that say quite clearly how early dinosaur-bone discoveries in China most likely created the whole dragon myth.

Mythology

You may have to start in the kids' section, but nearly every library has a decent mythology collection. Look for books like *Bulfinch's Mythology* or Edith Hamilton's book on the Greek myths (entitled *Mythology*), just to name a couple. If you're interested in comparative mythology—the similarities between myths and legends of different cultures—check out Joseph Campbell's books, particularly *The Hero with a Thousand Faces*. Campbell is not a good primary academic source, but his material is readable and will give you a basic understanding of how various archetypes are adapted to specific cultures. The librarian probably won't even give you a second glance if you're suddenly reading a lot of mythology books.

Studying world mythology also has another benefit if you haven't yet chosen—or, more accurately, been chosen by—a God or Goddess yet. The more mythology you know, the more likely you'll know your God and/or Goddess by name when they show up. It's nice to know someone's name when you first meet, isn't it?

Crafts

Your local drugstore or dollar store doesn't have the right color candles for your next Sabbat? There's probably a book in your library that can tell you how to make them. Want to make your own scented soap for a ritual bath? Look it up in the library.

If your Goddess would like you to learn how to spin yarn and then weave or knit it into something—there's probably a book for that, too. I have to admit that it is quite spiritually satisfying to sit and knit something warm for yourself or a loved one (or, better yet, for a charity), and it's a great way to connect with non-Pagan neighbors. You may run into trouble if you try to start an open Pagan discussion group in your town, but no one will blink if you and a group of non-Pagans meet regularly for a "Stitch and Bitch" afternoon. The other knitters, crocheters, cross-stitchers, etc. don't need to know you do what you do to honor a specific deity.

If your mother never taught you how to sew, the library is a good place to find a book to teach you how—unless, of course, you prefer to celebrate your rituals skyclad—i.e., nude. If you want ritual robes and really don't want to hire your Sunday school teacher who also happens to be the local seamstress to make them for you, a quick trip to the library for a book on sewing techniques and/or general needlework is probably in your future.

So don't automatically dismiss your library because it doesn't have that latest Pagan book your online friend highly recommended. There is enough information on the shelves already to satisfy and increase your spiritual minimum daily requirement for years to come if you know what to look for.

If Wishes Were Fishes

I believe I'm the only Pagan in my immediate town,
but I do have access to a shop in Baraboo, about fifteen

minutes away. It would be nice to have more people to talk to, but it is not a necessity for me.

—WITCH OF THE WOODS, MERRIMAC, WISCONSIN

In the survey, I asked what the respondents thought would enhance their overall Pagan practice that they didn't have access to in a small town. Not surprisingly, books, supplies, and other Pagans to talk to were the most popular answers.

I would love to have a little New Agey shop just up the street. Instead of paying out the bum for shipping from out of state or having to blow half a tank of gas just for lavender, I could just take my bike up the street, and voilà. I'm not a social creature, but it would be wonderful to meet with other Pagans in the area just to kick around ideas when the mood strikes. A bookstore, ANY kind of bookstore, would be a Goddess-send! The closest bookstore with a decent selection is across the border in Mishawaka, Indiana.

—RAVENNA, DOWAGIAC, MICHIGAN

I would love if there were more Pagan shops in this area so I didn't have to purchase online. It would definitely be much more "festive" to see more public celebrations of the seasonal festivals.

—DEANNA EBERLIN, ADDISON, NEW YORK

More people to discuss ideas with would definitely be nice. A more comprehensive recycling program

> *would help, too, since faith and enviro-consciousness*
> *intersect so solidly for me.*
>
> —BECCA, CLOVIS, NEW MEXICO

Even if the Emigrant doesn't need a great deal of contact with fellow Pagans to feel soul-fed, if he or she is accustomed to certain non-Pagan or Pagan-friendly activities that just aren't available in a small town, this could cause a problem. And sometimes the problem can escalate at minimum into a feeling of spiritual disconnectedness or at worse into a major personal religious crisis.

If, for example, attending or teaching dog-training classes is an important part of your religious expression and you move to a small town with no dog club for miles and don't feel you have the time or expertise to start your own, what do you do? Or suppose participation in a performance group of some kind (community theater, band, or chorus) was a big part of your connection to your deity back "home" in the big city and there's nothing in town that works as well for you— and you don't have the money, local contacts, or support to get your own group going. What do you do?

What you do is wait, be patient, and know that if these non-Pagan activities are truly what you need deep down in your soul, the opportunities to express yourself in something at least close to the ways you've been accustomed to will come to you—usually when you least expect them.

One example, and this one isn't pretty, nor is it easy for me to relate. Music, specifically the traditional songs of England and Appalachia, has always been a big part of my personal practice. *Nothing* feeds my soul like sitting around singing these songs with a group of people. It doesn't matter if they're Pagan or Christian—only the music matters to me. But now I live in a small town where there just aren't monthly folk sings, performance groups dedicated to this kind of music, or weekend folk dance events that include song workshops—all activities I was accustomed to growing up in Kentucky and then living in or near Washington, DC for so many years. In the past decade since I left the East Coast for love and starry skies in the Midwest, I haven't had as many opportunities to sing with others; in fact, I don't sing nearly as much as I'd like to, or as I should.

But the Gods will provide opportunities when it's important. Recently a beloved family member had major life-saving emergency surgery and, due to the fact that the surgery took place on Christmas Eve in the middle of an honest-to-Goddess blizzard (which followed an ice storm), I was the only loved one at the hospital. To say that this experience was a major test of my spiritual and emotional strength is an understatement. If you've been through something similar, you know what I mean and if you haven't been through something similar, nothing I say will adequately describe it to you. By the time the seven-hour operation was over and my family member was transferred to the intensive care unit, I was a bona fide physical, mental, and emotional wreck. And the only thing I could think of to do for my own mental health and to calm the patient (who was struggling to get rid of a breathing tube) was pull up a chair, take this person by the hand, and start singing.

I sat there and sang the English and Appalachian songs of my childhood—the only ones that were able to make their way to the forefront of my freaked-out brain—for about two hours, beeping machinery and bustling nurses notwithstanding. It wasn't the ideal situation in which to sit and create the music that means the most to me, but it worked—my soul was fed enough that I stayed more or less in one piece, my loved one was calmed by the music, and the energy of the songs got us through. I suspect that now that this "door" has been reopened, it will not close again. I've already found a way to keep it at least a little bit open, and found other people to sing with on a semi-regular basis.

Even so, if I had to say what I wish I had better access to for my own practice, it would be more family-friendly community events close by—concerts, coffee shops, discussion groups, and so forth. On the other hand, my family was recently invited to a "bonfire" at a Pagan friend's backyard in the next small town down the road. Most yards have them here—a small fire pit dug into the center of the yard, edged with broken bricks or large stones. We had a great time roasting hot dogs (and later marshmallows) over the flames, and just talking about a variety of Pagan and non-Pagan topics. It was cold for late May (we were all in sweatshirts and jackets), but the fire was warm, the company was congenial, and as the sky darkened we got to lean back and watch the stars come out. There's a lot less light pollution in small towns, and I saw more stars that night than I even knew existed. I had more than my minimum daily requirement of Pagan-ness that night. Would we have been able to have even a bonfire in the middle of a large city? Probably not.

Spirituality is not found in books, nor do more people make it any more accessible. Anything that I need, I have or can find easily enough.

—MOONDANCER, WASHINGTON STATE

Honestly? Perhaps because I am already well satisfied with my spirituality, I feel that living in a small town with greater access to nature has enhanced my practices more than anything else. Books can be ordered at my Pagan bookstore or online, and people either find their way to my doorstep or I go and find them. I love living in a small town. I like the neighbors that I have and the friends that I have made. They don't have to be Pagan to be friends.

—JULIA, EAST STROUDSBURG, PENNSYLVANIA

CHAPTER 6

Internetworking: Finding Others of Like Mind Online

I'm always swinging by Witchvox to look for shops within driving distance, festivals and meetups, local Pagans. Google isn't Pagan, but it's great for finding me what I need when I'm too lazy to link-hop. I am STRONG in the "Google-fu"! I don't have any other Pagan-ish sites that I visit regularly. I try to

> *bookmark good ones when I come across them, but*
> *then I rarely return. I just generally Google what I*
> *need, link-hop a while, and voilà.*
>
> —RAVENNA, DOWAGIAC, MICHIGAN

To say that the Internet has greatly helped Pagans in small towns—and big cities—connect with each other is like saying that the sun makes it easier to see during the day. Social networking sites such as Facebook, Myspace, and Twitter, and blogging sites like LiveJournal, make it easy to meet new friends and interact with others of a like mind without having to leave home.

For example, as of this writing I have over fifty friends on LiveJournal and about 120 friends on Myspace, plus the aforementioned 177 friends on Facebook. A handful of them are old college friends (and their spouses) and former co-workers; the rest are Pagans I've met online or in person at some time or other. When my family moved to Portales, New Mexico, and struggled unsuccessfully for four years to start a local networking community, discussion group, or coven, these online friends were our social and spiritual lifeline. The day we got DSL at home was my happiest day there. I finally felt like I could "talk" to my friends without waiting all afternoon for a webpage to load like it did on our old dial-up system.

Witchvox and Other Recommended Sites

Every single survey respondent, even the ones not quoted in these pages, mentioned Witchvox (www.witchvox.com), also known as the Witches' Voice, as the flagship site for Pagan contact and information on the Internet. There's a page for every state and many foreign countries, and each page includes listings for local events, study groups, covens, shops, Pagans offering services (tarot reading, house painting, web design, etc.), local Pagans in the news, and a list of Pagans in the state alphabetically by town or city. Witchvox also offers hundreds if not thousands of articles on pretty much every Pagan subject, a comprehensive list of Pagan books and magazines, and national and international news items of interest.

The survey respondents also recommended some smaller, more specific sites. Here are their—and my—favorites:

Yahoo Groups (groups.yahoo.com): If you're looking for local e-mail groups, Yahoo Groups seems to have the most. While living in Manitowoc, Wisconsin, I was able to connect with people in Milwaukee and Sheboygan through various Yahoo groups—often finding out about local events (Pagan Pride Days, drumming circles, Pagan picnics) that for whatever reason weren't listed on Witchvox.

There are also national and international Pagan Yahoo groups. For example, anyone interested in finding out more about British Traditional Wicca (Gardnerian, Alexandrian, Mohsian, Central Valley, Kingstone, among others) should check out the *Amber and Jet* Yahoo group.

Gay male Pagans may be interested in the Yahoo group *Brotherhood of the Phoenix*. The Yahoo group *naturalwitch* is very active and is a must-read for any Pagans interested in organic gardening, animal rights, natural remedies, recycling, and similar topics. There are also Yahoo groups for Pagan parents, solitaries, and even Pagans who are interested in scientifically based ghost hunting. There's also, incidentally, a Yahoo group called *Small Town Pagans*, a space for people who fit that description and want to hang out together. Needless to say, I see the moderator of that group quite often—every time I look in the mirror, in fact.

LiveJournal (www.livejournal.com): Although primarily a free blogging site, LiveJournal also offers quite a few Pagan communities where the members engage in intelligent, interesting discussion. The *Wiccan* and *Non-Fluffy Pagans* LiveJournal communities are both informative and lively, and *cr_r* for Celtic Reconstructionists is quite scholarly— just to name a few. There are some regionally based communities, usually by state, but they don't seem to have a lot of active members.

The Wild Hunt (www.wildhunt.org/blog): The Wild Hunt blog is the brainchild of Jason Pitzl-Waters, and covers national and international items of interest to Pagans. Jason is as good a news reporter as he is a news analyst (i.e., he's outstanding at both). I check it every day as part of my daily news-reading ritual because, hey, I'm a journalist, too!

Internet Sacred Text Archive (www.sacred-texts.com): This site hosts a huge collection of really interesting articles on every world religion, including Paganism. I spent an entire afternoon looking up some nifty, obscure Pagan stuff.

Myth*ing Links (www.mythinglinks.org): "An Annotated & Illustrated Collection of Worldwide Links to Mythologies, Fairy Tales & Folklore, Sacred Arts & Sacred Traditions." The site is a little confusing to navigate at first, but it's worth it.

Beliefnet (www.beliefnet.com): This site gives the basics of every world religion, including Paganism. Check out Beliefnet's own Pagan blogger, Gus diZerega, at http://blog .beliefnet.com/apagansblog. Gus's blog is also part of my daily news-reading ritual.

Cauldron Living (www.cauldronliving.com): There are some good articles and links to online covens here.

The Cauldron (www.ecauldron.com): The forums are run by pretty intelligent people, and the site comes highly recommended. If you want to "talk" to other Pagans, this is a good place to go.

Cybercovens

If chatting in online forums or tweeting your fellow Pagans on Twitter isn't giving you as much contact as you crave and there just aren't any other Pagans in your area, you might want to consider starting or joining a cybercoven. I've never been in a cybercoven and don't know anyone who has, but I do know the subject is somewhat controversial. The question at the heart of the debate is, "Can a ritual conducted electronically, with the participants hundreds, if not thousands, of miles apart, be 'real'?"

Because of my utter lack of experience in this matter, I consulted and interviewed an expert, Lisa McSherry. Lisa is a published author and is also the High Priestess of JaguarMoon Coven, a cybercoven that has been in existence since 2001. Whether you're a Hometowner or an Emigrant, I think at least parts of her story will sound familiar to you. No matter where you grew up, you may think cybercovens are the Internet's biggest joke and plan to stay far away from them, or you might believe cybercovens provide valid spiritual experiences and opportunities for growth for their members, and you're considering joining or starting one. Either way, I think you'll be interested in what Lisa ("LM" in our interview below) has to say.

> BF: *How do you feel the experiences of an online versus in-person coven differ, and how are they the same regarding learning, member's spiritual growth, and incidents of personal gnosis?*
>
> LM: The simplistic answer is that they are very similar, or can be, and each has its strengths and weaknesses. When I went about creating an online coven, I was operating off of the presumption that if it worked in the physical it will work in the virtual; you just need to think about it differently. For example, in physical ritual the ritual

leader can indicate participants' next movements silently—gesturing with a chalice, for example. Obviously that won't work online, and giving directions can be disconcerting to the poetry of the ritual. What we do is indicate in the text itself what the movements are and make it clear to participants that they are mirroring our actions on their own. This makes them active rather than passive, which can be a huge difference from physical ritual.

So the ritual might go as follows:

High Priestess: "Lord Herne, I stand before you and offer up the bounty of the season!"

Herne: "Your offering is welcome, my child. And in return I offer you my blessing."

*Herne places His hands on Maat's head.

The * is a marker from IRC [Internet Relay Chat], the program we use for real-time interactions, such as ritual or classes. And, yes, when we do ritual, someone aspects [draws down or becomes possessed by] the deities present. There are some very good examples in my book *The Virtual Pagan*.[14]

BF: *What is absolutely critical for a successful cybercoven?*

LM: Online groups need:

---

14. *The Virtual Pagan: Exploring Wicca and Paganism Through the Internet.* (Weiser Books, 2002).

- either a strong leader or a strong group of people with rotating leadership
- people who are comfortable communicating—silence is death online
- people who are comfortable expressing their needs and wants (and know the difference)

Online groups don't survive unless everyone is an adult, or willing to do the work to be an adult—that is why there are so few of them (relatively). A bright, communicative person says, "Let's form a coven, and we'll do it online." They accept every person who applies, have no structure, and don't have enough people to keep conversations going. The leader starts to feel overwhelmed because she's the only one posting topics, and hardly anyone is talking about them. No one wants to pitch in and plan rituals, but they'll gladly show up (not on time) at anything she puts together. There are 250 people in the group, but only five talk and they are all her friends. Is it any surprise they are gone in two years?

Leadership is not something most people are born to, and leading online is not easy. It's one reason I wrote a book about magickal group dynamics[15]—they are not like those found in typical group situations, like school or work.

---

15. *Magickal Connections: Creating a Lasting and Healthy Spiritual Group* (New Page Books, 2007).

Fundamentally, I think there is nothing that can't be done online that is done in physical groups. Our rituals are strong and successful. I initiate online, and it is as real as any physical initiation. The challenges are different, but one is no better than the other, as an absolute. It's a matter of which is better for the individual.

BF: *Without compromising their identity, how many of your members live in rural areas versus larger towns or cities?*

LM: Hmmm . . . I'm going to go with the entire history of JaguarMoon Coven and tell you that about 75 percent live outside of metropolitan areas. Overall, about 15 percent have lived in really rural settings (although that is a pretty flexible term).

BF: *What do you think draws a person to join an online coven?*

LM: It's a huge benefit for those who don't have a group anywhere near them. Many of my students and covenmates over the years have said that they just don't have another group to work with in their area. For those who are "disabled"— in a wheelchair, deaf, even blind—working online might be the only way they can get into a group. Each year we've had at least one student from out of the U.S.—Germany, France, Martinique, Australia, the U.K., just to name a few.

It's also anonymous. Dan the kindergarten teacher can more easily be Ravenwing the Witch online without fear of losing his job because someone saw him hanging out with other Witches. I've had a number of covenmates over the years who were in sensitive professions, where being a Witch was tantamount to being out of a job. Online, no one knows unless you tell them.

BF: *That brings up an interesting point. One of the ongoing issues for critics of the Internet is the anonymity it can provide. Anonymity can be a good thing for Dan the kindergarten teacher, but how do you know the people who ask to join JaguarMoon are who they really say they are? Have you had any trouble with "imposters"?*

LM: Anonymity is absolutely a two-sided issue. On the one hand, it's a protective mechanism, one that allows us to explore facets of our personality we might not otherwise allow to be public. On the other, it can be a way to promulgate negativity in a variety of ways.

BF: *I assume you mean "trolls"?*

LM: Yes. In JaguarMoon we just haven't had a lot of problems with it. For one thing, we encourage people to share as much, or as little, about their non-class thoughts/responses with others as they wish. So anonymity is a flexible, and protected, device. Moreover, by the time you join the coven, you've spent a year with us in a variety of situations—that is a long time to maintain falsehoods. It's not impossible, but where is the benefit? Magickal workings are energetic exchanges; we'd *notice* if something was consistently being held back, and we'd most likely let that person know that they aren't a good fit and wish them well on their journey elsewhere.

BF: *What about the other big Internet issue—minors having access to adult material? Most, if not all, legitimate face-to-face covens won't let anyone under the age of eighteen join unless their parents are members, too. How do you handle the fact that a minor can be perceived as an adult online?*

LM: The class and (by extension) the coven doesn't accept anyone under the age of twenty-one. It's too tough to manage if you aren't at a reasonably stable place in your life, with a fairly significant amount of personal control over your time, schedule, and (most of all) privacy. Our year-long class is a lot more like a graduate-level seminar than an undergraduate degree in terms of reading, writing, and discussion. Moreover, I have yet to meet a student who didn't experience profound change in their life while taking the class. From my perspective, it is as if they say to the Universe, "I want to be a Witch," and the Universe says, "Okay. You've got to get rid of the stuff that holds you back from self-evolution.

Here, let me take care of it for you." I'm not saying it's guaranteed, but it is absolutely typical.

BF: *And you're saying teenagers aren't likely to handle getting rid of their "stuff"?*

LM: Right! I suppose that if someone lied and said they were old enough to join the class, I wouldn't have any way to verify it one way or another. But I think they'd just drop out because it's too tough. If they are a minor living at home, it's unlikely they could get enough private time to meditate, do classwork, attend rituals and our "live" classes. If they are on their own, ages eighteen to twenty-one is a very busy time for most people. I'd guess they just drop out, and hopefully return in a few years.

We screen by asking for mundane name, address, and birthdate as a part of the application process. Like I said: they can lie about all of that, but what would the point be? If they are good enough to join the coven after the class, they are stuck maintaining a lie that would become more and more difficult to sustain as time goes on and personal evolution occurs. If not—then, they have proved themselves to be an exception. And then what?

Lying is ultimately a waste of resources and energy, and is incredibly self-defeating. We presume people are telling the truth and let it all work out.

BF: *Do you see online covens as a spiritually viable choice for people who live in tiny towns that are too far away from urban centers to realistically meet folks of a like mind? Why or why not?*

LM: Absolutely! If there is a local group, you may not like the people in it—this is true even in urban areas. If you're in the "Bible Belt" (which is a pretty big area of the United States), then it might be impossible to find anyone of even a vaguely like mind in your community.

Other Online Groups

Not all online spiritual groups follow a coven structure—i.e., training new students, celebrating the eight Sabbats and full moons together, or initiating worthy candidates. Ruth Merriam has a face-to-face coven that she is very involved with, but she also works with an online group dedicated to the goddess Brigid. I asked her about her unique perspective in comparing the two experiences. If you don't want an online coven but would like to be in cybercontact with other devotees of your chosen deity, this may inspire you to start a similar group.

BF: *Tell me a little about your Brigid group.*

RM: It started as a brainchild of someone else that I knew on LiveJournal. We started as a LiveJournal community, but it didn't go anywhere so we switched over to a Yahoo group.

Right now there are twenty-four women in the group. As per the nuns who follow Brigid, or St. Bridget, at Kildare, Ireland, we have set up a twenty-day rotation of tending a flame in honor and worship of Brigid. We tend a flame nineteen of the days, and on the twentieth day Brigid tends it Herself. The vigil takes place from sundown to sundown. When a woman first joins the group, she receives a special candle that she can use to light the flame and instructions on how to re-create the special candle when that one is gone.

BF: *How active is the Yahoo group?*

RM: There's not a lot of talk in the group. There's a real sense of silent sisterhood—I know that my sisters are doing their job; it's a palpable feeling when the sister who has the vigil before me finishes and I am to begin.

Depending on membership, some women do more than one vigil per twenty-day period. Occasionally some of us will talk about personal stuff through the Yahoo group, but it's very much a personal practice with a group source.

It's not a coven—anyone can do this. Anyone can set up a group to worship a particular deity.

In addition to flame-tending, some of us make and exchange biddy dolls—made of corn husks or rags—at Imbolc. The dolls bless the recipient's home in the coming year, and at the end of the year the doll is burnt. I started doing this in 1987 by making Brigid crosses, then slowly started making biddy dolls. I brought the idea to this group, and it's very effective.

BF: *What made you decide to join this group?*

RM: I'd already had a prior attachment with the biddy dolls when my friend came up with the flame sisters idea. I suggested we formalize it—we started with just a few women. The number ebbs and flows, which is fine.

BF: *If there had been a face-to-face group doing the same thing close to you, would you have joined that instead? Why or why not?*

RM: Probably not. I've got so many other parts of my Craft life that are face to face. The cyberspace nature of this forum is ideal for me. I'd love to meet some of the women in person someday, though.

BF: *What do you feel are the advantages to being in this group?*

RM: The personal, quiet aspect. It allows a connection and a commitment that doesn't require scheduling. This is something you don't necessarily have to schedule—if you can't physically light your flame at the beginning of your shift (sundown), you can meditate on it and light it in your heart.

For some women, it's the only time they give themselves permission to sit quietly and light a candle and nothing else.

BF: *That's rather sad.*

RM: Yes, it is. But it gives them that joyful obligation to take time for devotion.

BF: *The group is all women, then?*

RM: Oh, yes.

BF: *How do you enforce that?*

RM: With very few exceptions, all of the women in the group were recommended by someone already in the group—either they knew the candidate personally or had corresponded with her for many years.

BF: *And this referral system also takes care of the potential for an underage person joining?*

RM: Absolutely.

BF: *Are there any disadvantages to how the group is set up— personal commitment coupled with an online component?*

RM: I can speak as the moderator of the group. It's occasionally difficult to have the utmost faith to know that the women are doing what they say they are doing. Some only check in every six months. Without regular face-to-face or phone contact, I have to take it on faith that the women are keeping their scheduled vigils.

Other than that, there are no more problems than you'd find in any other online group. We had one woman who was a bit of a drama queen, but we only had to talk to her about it once. It's very self-policing and by far the easiest Pagan group I've been involved with.

BF: *How experienced are your members? I'd imagine that you'd have to have a basic working knowledge of Pagan practice and be pretty comfortable with it in order to participate meaningfully.*

RM: Actually, they range. There are some that are what I call *Paganesque*—they've not had any formal training or group practice. Others have a variety of training and experience. I think one woman is Christian and does this as worship to St. Bridget.

BF: *What do you get out of it, spiritually speaking?*

RM: I moved relatively recently, and now I don't have the long-standing ties and connections with the people in my "place." As you get older, it's harder to make those connections; I don't have a school-age child, I don't work outside the home, and of course I don't go to church. I'm used to working with a small group of people, but that doesn't mean I like to be isolated.

This group is more than just electrons. The flame I tend—there is a sense of community, a sense in this small cadre of women that we are doing something that matters. It's a quiet, reflective thing.

For me, it provides the motivation to do what Brigid wants me to do. There are a lot of projects that I'm always working on at home—sewing, paperwork, etc. For a long time, I'd move my little red oil lamp that I light for my vigil every time it was my turn. There was always a project going on all around it. I don't do that anymore. Now I see the lamp as Brigid giving me a kick in the ass to take care of business. So as I work on these things, I speak to Her and She to me.

Discussion Groups

There are also even more informal Pagan groups on the Internet for people who don't feel ready for coven work or can't find—or don't want to create—a group dedicated to their particular deity. I asked my friend and former "in-person" student Cordelia about her experiences with online study groups.

BF: *Why did you join an online study group?*

C: Theoretically, I was in a couple of them. The first one was a Yahoo group, and it was more of a community—not very intensive. It was more varied, and we used it more as a discussion group than anything else. Then one of the women on the list privately e-mailed her phone number to some of us, asking if we wanted to do something more intensive. We tried to have a cybercoven. It lasted a couple of years before it fizzled out.

BF: *Can you describe some of your experiences in that group, both positive and negative?*

C: We did rituals via e-mail. They didn't do anything, but they were pretty harmless. We all tried to out-pretty each other writing invocations to the four quarters. It was a good exercise in creative writing!

Sometimes we'd pick a night and all meditate at the same time, and then the next morning we'd post our experiences to the group.

One member was sixteen years old. I don't remember anyone making an issue of her age. If we'd had more sense, we might have worried about it.

BF: *Were there minimum posting requirements? Did you have to post daily or weekly or whatever to be a member in good standing or anything like that?*

C: It might have been better if there had been posting requirements. Some—half—never posted much. If there'd been more structure, it would have been better.

BF: *Why did you leave, or did you leave?*

C: It kind of died. The woman in charge tried to make a smaller group later—I was one of the people she picked. There were four people in that new group; two of them never posted anything. We tried to continue, to share the results of our simultaneous meditations. I'm still friends with two of the people from that group.

BF: *What made you decide to join an online Pagan group?*

C: I liked the people. I wanted to belong to a group, and there was nothing really local to me. I thought, "These are people I like; we're like-minded and can discuss things." Calling it a "coven" made it glamorous.

BF: *How did your online group experience compare to being a member of a face-to-face group?*

C: You definitely raise more energy face to face. Also, the people you're dealing with are really the people you're dealing with; there's no chance for deception. Real-life covens end, not just fizzle out.

BF: *Who do you think is best served by a cybercoven?*

C: People who are really shy or really out in the boondocks. Especially people who are shy, since they're not comfortable going out and meeting others.

I appreciated the lessons and learning in the face-to-face coven I was a member of. We were going to have lessons in the online group, but we never did. About half the group had a couple years' experience, and the other half were complete newbies. I guess we were supposed to expound about our knowledge or something [*laughs*], but we weren't comfortable doing that because we hadn't been doing it for very long ourselves.

Things to Consider about Online Groups

As I mentioned, there is a great deal of debate within the Pagan community as to whether cybercovens and online study or discussion groups "work" at all, with opponents saying that you *must* interact with people face to face or you're simply engaging in mental "fluff" and deluding yourself.

It's also a basic fact that cybercovens and online discussion groups will not work for everyone. During my recent undergraduate career, I took online courses and in-the-classroom courses—often in the same semester and with the same professors teaching in both forums. Maybe it's just my own personal learning style, but I retained more from the in-person classes than I did the online ones. I learn better in a "hands-on" environment. If this is true for you as well, an online group or coven would probably not be a good fit for you.

There are also some things that are hard—some would say impossible—to learn "virtually." Energy work is often cited as one of these, as is learning how to draw down—i.e., serve as a channel for divine possession. If anything falls under the category "don't try this at home alone," it's drawing down. I don't want to scare you or discourage you from experiencing the awesome opportunity to literally become one with a god or goddess, but (and this is a *big* "but") for your own safety and continuing good mental health, do not try to learn how to draw down from a book or the Internet. For all you know, the faceless online person teaching you how to draw down may not have the first clue how to really do it, or many not even be who—and what, credentially speaking—they say they are.

In addition to anonymity issues, detractors of online study groups and cybercovens cite the lack of group cohesion as another reason why virtual groups don't work. Their theory is that forming the interpersonal bonds necessary to create a group mind or group gestalt is impossible when the group members are not only scattered all over the country but have also never even seen each other face to face. I am cautiously neutral on this issue. As a veteran of the halcyon days of the popularity of Internet Relay Chat (the "IRC" Lisa McSherry mentioned) in the mid-to-late 1990s, I have to admit that I did form a bond with my fellow regulars in various chat rooms. These were not Pagan venues per se (one was a writer's critique group), but our time together in the chat rooms and/or on the phone with each other felt real. I followed their life problems and trials on IRC and they helped me with mine, just as in-person friends and acquaintances would. It may have all been in my head, but to me—and I think to the other regulars—it was all very, very real. So I'm willing to agree that a sense of group cohesion and some sort of group mind is *possible* over the Internet.

However, I have to agree with the critics who say that it is not possible for a cybergroup to raise energy. Yes, Ruth Merriam said that she could feel "when the sister who has the vigil before me finishes and I am to begin," but that is not the same thing. In order to learn and feel how to raise and use group energy—also sometimes referred to as a Cone of Power—you need, well, a group.

In general, though, I advocate a good online study group or cybercoven over no group experience at all. And by "good," I mean: focused, mostly free of drama, with a knowledgeable leader or leaders, and one that has not been formed last week or by high school students.

It might also be wise to consider Moondancer's answer to the survey question "What Pagan-oriented sites on the Internet do you recommend for shopping, networking, information, etc.?":

> *For the most part, I don't. I check www.witchvox .com every week or so and subscribe to a number of Pagan lists, but, frankly, most of them are not worth the time it takes to hit the delete key. Get involved in your local gardening club or book discussion group. Be with people, not the computer.*

---------- CHAPTER 7 ----------

Community Building

We began a PNO, advertising on Meetup (useless),
Witchvox (limited success), and with posters at the
Chaplain Center on base (complicated). It's been a
cycle of ups and downs for years.

—NOEY, COUPEVILLE, WASHINGTON

As Noey indicates, it's tough to organize a regular in-person
(as opposed to online) Pagan group. More than one experienced Pagan leader has likened the process to "herding cats"
or "wrangling butterflies." Organizing any sort of Pagan
group can be even harder in a small town, where meeting

places are few and far between and potential members are relatively scarce.

When asked if they had ever tried to start, or had successfully started, a discussion group/meetup or ritual-oriented group like a coven, most survey respondents replied, "No." Some took it a step further: *"Hell* no" was a common comment.

But other survey respondents said they would think about it, and a few even commented that they had no clue how to even begin to gather together those of like mind and compatible zip codes.

Starting Your Own Discussion Group, Study Group, or PNO (Pagan Night Out)

Discussion groups, study groups, and Pagan Nights Out (PNOs) are a good way for newcomers to, or those interested in, Paganism to learn a little bit more in a friendly environment that, unlike a coven or study group, requires no commitment whatsoever. These get-togethers are also a great way for potential leaders—i.e., you—to start researching and presenting informal lectures on topics near and dear to your heart. A PNO does not necessarily have to take place in the evening; it's just a term for Pagans coming together at a scheduled time in a public place to chat and share ideas—and because Pagans are involved, food usually is, too.

> *I've been to one ritual here in Bakersfield, and it left much to be desired. As sad as that is, there was*

> *no energy in the ritual whatsoever. I see people in*
> *my town wearing pentacles and they always just*
> *come up to me with big smiles and say, "Blessed Be"*
> *or something similar. At the moment there are no*
> *meetups, because the person who was running them*
> *here left town.*
>
> —SPIRITRUNNER, BAKERSFIELD, CALIFORNIA
> (PREVIOUSLY IN TAFT, CALIFORNIA)

I believe we could use a lot more of these informal groups, and I mean a *lot*. I recently took a quick glance at a few states' Witchvox pages (including that of my own state, Kansas). There are so many (too many) small-to-medium-sized towns that are home to a dozen or so Pagans, but unless someone in the area feels qualified to organize anything, there is no venue for these folks to get together. So they don't. And the opportunity to connect, to share information and ideas and feel like part of a community, is lost.

Feeling like part of an ongoing community is very important. I recently facilitated a discussion at a major Pagan festival about life as a small-town Pagan. The discussion / workshop was very well attended, and while I was more or less prepared for the "us vs. them" feelings the participants expressed as they recounted stories about the pressure they feel at home to join a specific church, I was not at all prepared for the pain I heard in the attendees' voices as they talked about the isolation they feel from their "tribe" during the fifty-one weeks of the year when they weren't at this particular Pagan gathering. But, like my survey respondents, most of the workshop participants were either too frightened or didn't feel qualified to start their own discussion group, book club, or even regular, open non-Pagan drumming/bonfire event.

This is what I told the discussion attendees that day. I hope it helps you, too:

Starting your own group or event takes a lot of patience while membership slowly builds. The woman who started the weekly Pagan discussion group in Sheboygan, Wisconsin, sat in the meeting space all by herself every Tuesday for several weeks waiting for others to join her. But she had to; odds are good that the one time she didn't go was the one time a potential member would show up.

Starting your own book discussion group or meetup also takes perseverance. Depending on the size of, and attitudes in, your town, there are probably very few venues willing to host a Pagan discussion group or ritual (more on this in a moment). Plus, how willing are you to be at least semi if not fully out of the broom closet by starting your own group or event?

For Hometowners who are trying to keep their new religion out of the local spotlight, this may be the biggest deterrent. Emigrants, who are just trying to fit in on a number of social, political, and/or cultural levels, may not want to "rock the boat" further by starting a group—even though they may be the ones most comfortable and happy attending at least a PNO on a fairly regular basis. Both Hometowners and Emigrants will have to look very carefully at how their job and/or family (especially school-age children) could be negatively affected by such public exposure.[16] And by public exposure I mean Pagan and non-Pagan public—how "out" are you willing to be, not only to your fellow Pagans whom you may or may not know, but also to your neighbors; co-workers; and (for Hometowners) old, non-Pagan friends?

This is not a small issue. A dear friend of mine in Columbia, Missouri, took over organizing the monthly discussion group and annual Pagan Pride Day event, which, of course, made her visible enough to the local media that she became the one they called for the required Halloween article and, of course, was the one to talk to on Pagan Pride Day. Despite her requests that the reporters only print her Pagan name, eventually one did not honor that request and she was instantly outed. Unfortunately, my friend was an elementary school teacher and lost her job. She took a chance, decided the organizing needed to happen so the Pagans in her town could connect—and lost her livelihood as a result.

But most of all, starting your own Pagan Night Out or study group takes a fair amount of confidence in your own knowledge and your ability to share that knowledge with others. You have to believe that, while you may not be an expert on every possible Pagan subject, you know just enough about a variety of topics to at least facilitate a discussion on that topic and/or be able to know where to go to research the subject enough to organize a couple hours' talk on it. A lot of Pagans, even those who live in big cities, don't feel like they know enough to run such a group, so don't feel bad

16. Family and work issues will be discussed in depth in chapter 8.

if you think you don't know anything—you're not the only one!

I am certainly no exception to this. Just off the top of my head, I can come up with several basic Pagan topics I know next to nothing about, certainly not enough to discuss for two hours. This list includes astrology, herbalism, drumming (for all my folk-dancing background, I have *no* sense of percussive rhythm), runes, palmistry, planting a garden according to moon phases, massage, kitchen Witchery (cooking is what I do to food to make it edible and no more), Irish mythology, healing, and faeries. Trust me when I say that this is not a complete list!

Yet to date I have co-founded an entire umbrella community organization that includes one of the largest gatherings on the East Coast and organized/led the following: one smaller Pagan gathering, four covens, two study groups, two online networking groups, and one monthly PNO—all with varying degrees of success—oh, and written a ream of articles and (including this one) three books about Paganism. You don't have to know everything about everything; as long as you know enough about a couple of favorite topics, you'll be fine.

If you've decided you're determined enough, brave enough, out of the broom closet enough, and have good Internet or library research skills for topics you don't know that much about, here are the practical nuts and bolts for starting your own informal, non-coven group:

The first thing you need to do is decide how often you want to meet. Once a month is probably best for a book discussion group because your members will need the time in between meetings to, well, read the book. For general discussion, networking, or study groups, I recommend once a week, especially if there is nothing else Pagan-y going on in your town. Why? Because people who have heard about the meeting or have seen it posted are more likely to check it out if it's every week. They may miss this week, and even next week, but the week after that they remember in time to actually attend. If your PNO meets the second Tuesday of the month, for example, your potential attendees are more likely to forget which Tuesday this is, and will be less likely to show up.

The next thing you'll need, obviously, is a place to meet. If you have Unitarians, a Unity congregation, or Quakers in your town who have their own meeting space, you are in luck. You may have to attend their (Unitarian or Unity) services or (Quaker) meetings for a while so they get to know you. In my experience, a typical Sunday morning Unitarian service ranges from practically Pagan to spiritually neutral; you're not likely to feel uncomfortable. A Sunday morning Quaker meeting mostly consists of people sitting together in silence, much as they would at a Buddhist temple, although occasionally someone will feel "moved by the Spirit" to get up and say something. I am not Quaker, but I have attended several meetings. I've always found that when someone is moved to speak, their words are relevant to what's going on in my life.

Once you are comfortable with the Unitarians and/ or Quakers, casually ask if you could use their space for a weekly discussion group. Be honest and tell them what the discussion is to be about—i.e., things Pagan. Offer to accept small monetary donations from the discussion attendees to cover the cost of utilities your PNO will use (lights, heat, water) during the meeting. Promise you will not do Pagan ritual in their sacred space. If the Quakers or Unitarians say no, respect their answer and move on.

If you don't have Quakers or Unitarians in your town or you're not comfortable working with them, you will need to find a more secular year-round place to meet. Unless you live in a part of the country that has perfect outdoor weather 365 days of the year, that place needs to be inside—moving the meeting back and forth between a park in the summer and an indoor location in the winter is going to confuse potential members, and likely cause them to miss meetings.

Many Pagans host regular get-togethers and classes at the local public library, where meeting rooms are often available for free (or for a nominal fee) for non-profit groups. The only problem is, you will likely want to have your meeting in the evening (after people have gotten off work) and/or on the weekend, and many small-town libraries close for the day at 5:00 p.m. and are not open on the weekend at all. Check with your library, though. Sometimes they will have evening hours once or twice during the week. As long as you are not charging any sort of entry or attendance fee, the library should be okay with your group meeting there.

Some small towns have colleges; my town, Baldwin City, Kansas (population 4,401), does. See if you can find someone sympathetic who is a student or employee of the college, because the school will likely make a classroom available for free for your group to meet in with this person's help and sponsorship. Check the history, anthropology, or women's studies departments. If the college doesn't have a women's studies department, check the curriculum catalogue—usually available for viewing on the college's website—and see if any women's studies or women's literature classes are offered as part of the sociology or English departments, respectively, and talk to that professor.

Do not, I repeat, *do not* think about hosting the regular meetings of an open group in your home. Newcomers to Paganism won't feel comfortable going to a stranger's house and, really, how comfortable are you with people you don't know or don't know well coming to your home in a Pagan context?

Your best bet if there are no welcoming churches or colleges in your town is a restaurant or coffee shop, one that is either very busy so no one can hear well enough to eavesdrop on your group's discussion or one that has little to no business so there's no one else there to eavesdrop on your group's discussion. I recommend *against* buffet-type restaurants where attendees must pay for a meal to get in the door whether they eat anything or not. Some folks can't afford it (especially if there are children involved) or have dietary restrictions—vegetarian, vegan, or food allergies—and can't eat the buffet fare.

My favorite PNO site was a pizza place, where even though there were tables and booths in the restaurant, about 90 percent of its business was delivery. Hardly anyone ever ate there, so we pretty much had the place to ourselves. You didn't have to order anything, and a glass of ice water was free. The manager was tickled to bits to have ten to twenty people regularly show up at his restaurant and, at minimum, order a soft drink. If he'd had his way, we'd have been there every night, and just so at least half of us kept ordering food and drink, he could have cared less about our obvious jewelry and topics of discussion.

Some chain restaurants like Perkins and Denny's have private or semi-private back rooms available for group use, but you need to reserve them in advance and make it clear in your publicity what "name" the reservation is under. If you find out that the management is reluctant to send people who ask for your party to the back meeting room, or if somehow the reservation you made three weeks in advance is almost always "lost" (or if the manager tells you, "Oh, another group is using the room"), realize that the restaurant is trying to tell you something: your group is not welcome. Move on.

Speaking of publicity, this is your next hurdle. Unless you are ready to personally assume a minimum of twelve dollars per month in fees or strongly request (demand) a small financial commitment from your attendees, I recommend against using the services of Meetup.com. Yes, Meetup will send out the lovely reminder e-mails for you, but you can do that yourself for free.

Fortunately, there are cheap (i.e., free) ways to get the word out about your group. Witchvox.com, of course, is a must-post place for your PNO information. If people in your town and the next town over have a personal listing on

Witchvox that says they are open to invites, send out an e-mail. You don't have to say much, just a quick "Hi, I'm starting a discussion group. We meet every Wednesday at 7:00 at such-and-such location. You're welcome to come, and if you have any topic ideas for future meetings, let me know!" You can also send a similar message to people who are on Myspace and live close to you. You don't even need to friend them first. If you know of semi-local Pagans through Facebook or Twitter, send them a notice, too. It's free!

Check and see if there are any Yahoo or Google e-mail groups that cover your town. Even if you are an hour or more away from a big city that does have a Yahoo group, join it—you never know who else in your town is a member. Post polite, *occasional* reminders and updates about your PNO and remember that this is not your personal publicity e-mail list. If there are no Yahoo e-mail groups in your area, consider starting one. It's free and easy; if I can start one, so can you!

Informal bulletin boards or information kiosks at your local college are also good places to post a flyer about your group. College students are often curious about religions other than the one they grew up in. Since these boards and kiosks are often outdoors, you may want to place your flyer in a clear plastic sheet protector first. Also, make plans to re-post your flyer every month or so—some college students are curious; others are also pretty strong in the faith of their childhood and may feel the need to tear down your flyer.

See if you can have a notice about your PNO or discussion group listed in the religion section or community calendar page of your local newspaper. Some editors won't allow it, but others may surprise you—you won't know until you ask. If you have a Unitarian church or fellowship in town, even if you're not meeting in their space, ask if you can post a flyer on their bulletin board or have a notice listed in their newsletter or on their website.

Do you have a natural food store or food co-op in town? Ask if you can post a flyer there—many Pagans are "into" the teas, herbs, "green" cleaning supplies, and cruelty-free hygiene products that natural food stores sell. They'll see your flyer the next time they need to stock up on sage or organic produce.

The flyers are posted; your Witchvox notice is getting hits; what do you do now? You put on as much Pagan-identifying jewelry as you're comfortable with, go to the meeting place at the regularly scheduled time, take a book or magazine (or in my case, knitting) to keep you entertained, and you sit. And sit. And sit. Make a list of topics while you sit and include a brief discussion outline for each one—it's good to be prepared for the day that someone actually comes.

As I mentioned earlier, the local PNO coordinator in Sheboygan, Wisconsin, sat alone every Tuesday for at least a couple of months before anyone else showed up. But show up they did, and now they've not only got a lively weekly discussion going, but the group also collectively decided to start a small, local Pagan festival that had about twenty-five attendees the first year. Not bad for a town where, just a few months earlier, the Pagans didn't even know each other.

You've Got Them, Now Keep Them

The key to having a good open group is to be flex-
ible. One of the best tools we have found for our
discussion book is question-and-answer night.
Everyone writes down a question, and we put the
questions in a box; then, as each question is drawn
out of the book, the entire group discusses it. It's
actually a great learning tool. The biggest pitfall
of running a discussion group? If you allow one
or two people's personal drama to come into the
group, it will destroy a group faster than anything.

—JULIA, EAST STROUDSBURG, PENNSYLVANIA

Once people start coming to your discussion group, what do
you do? How do you start each meeting? How do you keep
their interest? How do you handle the inevitable personality
clashes that come up?

At the beginning of each meeting, devote a few minutes
for introductions—name, Pagan path, some spiritual history—and if your group has a short list of rules (no inter-
rupting, speak respectfully, try to stay on topic, and so on), go
over them. Then start talking about this week's topic. Make a
note of other subjects or tangents that come up in the discussion—they may make great topics for future meetings.

As Julia hints at in the quote above, the best way to keep
people coming back to your weekly event is to offer a variety
of information in as many different formats as you can. Just
because your personal practice is primarily Celtic or British

in influence doesn't mean others in your group wouldn't be interested in information about the Greek and Roman pantheons. Invite regulars to your group to present or facilitate on a topic they know well. You don't always have to be the person leading the discussion—but have a backup topic ready in case at the last minute they don't show up.

See if you can find knowledgeable guests to come to your meeting and talk about their area of expertise—a local college is full of professors who know a great deal about Egyptian history, mythological motifs in Victorian art and literature, how to make your own ink, how to identify birds indigenous to your area, and a variety of other topics of interest to the members of your group. If you have a paranormal investigation group in your area, invite them to come and present some of the evidence they've collected (the closer to Samhain you can schedule this, the better!). See if the local wildlife or raptor rescue organization can bring some of their animals to at least part of your meeting and talk about the animals. We did this one just for kicks at the gathering I helped start in Maryland, and it quickly became one of the most popular parts of the festival for kids and adults alike—and the wildlife rescue group's donation box was always full when they left, which means they loved coming as much as we loved having them there.

Alternate hands-on "workshops" with discussion sessions. If you or another group member are good at reading tarot or working with pendulums or energy-sensing, don't just talk about it—do it!

If you can offer basic refreshments, even if it's hot water for tea or hot chocolate and a plate of store-bought cookies, do so. People in general and Pagans in particular like to eat, and hot tea is particularly "homey" and welcoming in cold weather.

Use various media to help get your point across. The leader of the Sheboygan weekly PNO devoted an entire week's session showing the movie *The Craft* to inspire discussion about Pagan ethics. I'm assuming she used the film as a cautionary example of how not to conduct your magical affairs. If your local movie-rental place doesn't carry *The Craft*, consider showing *Gladiator* (horribly historically inaccurate, but handles the Roman tradition of family gods quite well) or *The Lion King* (excellent way to illustrate the winter/summer, Lugh/Balor, Oak King/Holly King conflict) instead.

And then there's the inevitable conflict. One group member doesn't like one of the others; one dominates the conversation; another one gives off squicky vibes and is driving some of the other attendees away. What do you do?

Encourage the members who don't like each other to work it out themselves, or at least keep hostilities to a minimum during the weekly meeting. If one party can and the other one can't, ask the one that can't to leave. If the conflict is causing that much disruption, you're doing the group a favor, believe me.

Attendees who dominate the conversation, always seem to take the subject off track, or interrupt others can almost always be curbed by some basic group rules about limited talk or comment time, staying focused, and only speaking when others are not. A "talking stick" is particularly useful for stopping interrupters in their tracks. If they don't have the stick—or Buddha statue, or magical mystery tea mug, or whatever you choose the object to be—they have to stay quiet; it's as simple as that.

Unfortunately, Squicky Vibe Person is going to be the toughest one to deal with. You have to be very, very careful when dealing with this sort of problem. The trick is to make absolutely, positively sure that the person truly is projecting a presence that most everyone else, and not just one person, finds objectionable. We had this problem in the Sheboygan weekly group when, after months of just the leader and one other member attending every week, a young man joined about the same time I did. He made that other member quite nervous, and once she did some checking into his criminal background, the rest of us were nervous as well. Not that he'd done anything truly horrendous, but enough to garner a record.

The longtime member wanted the young man out. The rest of us (a couple more people had joined by the time this issue came to a head) were in "let's wait and see what he does" mode. The leader handled it beautifully. She spoke with the young man and with the longtime member separately. It turned out that the longtime member resented having to "share" the group with the rest of us—up until I and the young man showed up, she'd had this private Paganism 101 class going and she did not want to give that up. I knew too much about the topic near and dear to this woman's heart—Pagan practice—for her to want to get rid of me;

she'd apparently decided I was valuable. That left the young man, who eventually decided we were all too old and boring for his tastes. They both ended up wandering away from the group. Problem solved.

As your discussion group, book club, or meetup evolves, a core group of members will develop; don't be afraid to ask for their advice and input when your own unique interpersonal problems arise.

Of course, it's not always this easy, as some survey respondents reminded me.

> *I did try to start a discussion group to work each quarter with a different element. People came and went. Then just lost interest or got busy with other things.*
>
> —K, SEVIERVILLE, TENNESSEE

> *In high school we had a group that got together once a week to discuss stuff and have a small circle. It lasted about a year or so, then people either became overly busy or uninterested.*
>
> —SPIRITRUNNER, BAKERSFIELD, CALIFORNIA
> (FORMERLY IN TAFT, CALIFORNIA)

> *In high school, after seeing all the hype about the "prayer around the flagpole," I wanted to start up something for all the rest of the kids who weren't Christian, who wanted to explore outside the Bible box. It ended up being just myself and two close*

friends who got together to study, read cards, chant,
and hold circles. This only lasted a couple of years,
though.

—RAVENNA, DOWAGIAC, MICHIGAN

Going More Formal: Starting a Coven

If your discussion group is going well, yet there seems to be an "inner" group of people who get along well and want to try to celebrate the Sabbats together, then the role of coven leader may be in your future.

First and foremost, before you actually decide to form a group together, try doing a couple of rituals as a group first. Who knows, you might prefer quiet, meditative circles, while the other members like to drum and dance. You may prefer to plan and organize every Sabbat to a T—up to and including ten- to fifteen-page scripts that include every word of the ritual to pass out to every attendee, while your fellow discussion group members might prefer spontaneous, off-the-cuff rituals that follow a basic sequential outline that looks something like this, if this much: (1) Cast the circle; (2) Call the quarters; (3) Invoke the God and Goddess (which ones? We'll know when we get to that part!), (4) Do the actual ritual—celebrate Lammas, do a full moon meditation, etc., however it feels right; (5) Cakes and wine; (6) Dismiss the God and Goddess, quarters, and circle; (7) Eat potluck food until we drop.

As I mentioned in the ritual etiquette section in chapter 2, there's nothing at all wrong with different styles of ritual;

you just want to make sure as early as possible that everyone's preferred ritual forms are compatible *before* you formally create a coven. You will save yourself much heartache and many headaches if you do.

The publicity and organizational problems that accompany starting a discussion group still apply when you're starting a coven, and the solutions I've suggested for meetups should work when you're creating a more formal, committed unit. However, you need to know that running a ritual group has its own unique set of headaches that you must consider. Here are some questions you need to ask yourself—and honestly answer—before you commit to taking on this huge responsibility:

How good am I at forming group cohesion?

The phrase "It's like herding cats," which I referred to at the beginning of this chapter, was probably first coined by a coven leader. If it wasn't, it should have been! Pagans tend to be independent of thought, strong in their opinions, and just plain stubborn when it comes to matters of religious expression. Trying to get a group of these sorts of folk to agree on anything, much less trust each other in order to create group gestalt, would try the patience of a Buddhist monk. If you've been mediating conflict pretty well in your discussion group, you should be prepared to do what it takes (whatever that is for your specific group) to help your members work together in a highly focused setting.

Does this mean enough to me that I will commit to this for the long haul, or do I just want to be important?

A coven must meet, minimally, eight times a year for the holidays. Once you include full moon rituals and twice-monthly classes, that number swells to forty-five times a year, which is pretty darn close to once a week. Running a coven means you have to schedule the rest of your life around the group's schedule. You can't be a coven leader and say, "Oh, I won't be at Beltane, even though it's supposed to be at my house, because I'm taking my family camping." No. You have to be available for every single coven get-together. Vacations, family reunions, even an afternoon movie and dinner afterward with your spouse *all* have to take second place. And with a good coven lasting five to fifteen years, that's a long time to put off visiting your mom in the next state over on a "free weekend."

I once attended a ritual at which the host for that particular holiday was not going to be home until about five minutes before the ritual was supposed to start—his daughter had a dance recital that day. We all showed up anyway, and there was someone to let us in, but of course the recital ran late and of course that meant the ritual started late, too—by at least an hour and a half. What should the host have done? Trying to find an alternative site for the ritual, one where the host(s) would be home all day, would have been a good start. If the calendar on your wall is already full of family obligations, you may want to rethink starting a coven.

How many hot meals am I ready to miss?

It sounds trivial, but there were some periods with my students when there would be an emotional emergency or crisis of conscience every night around suppertime for four or five days in a row. I ate a lot of formerly hot food at those times, since it's rude to audibly chew your dinner in the ear of someone who is sobbing hysterically—at least it is where I come from. If mealtime is your special time with your significant other or family and you want to lead a coven, turn the phone off until the dishes are done and the leftovers are safely packed away.

Is my home usually clean enough to have rituals in?

If you're the leader, chances are your home will double as the covenstead. Fairly or unfairly, the filthier the home, the less likely your fellow coveners will take you seriously, much less want to come over to your house. I don't mean moderately cluttered, and I am not suggesting your living room/family room has to look like something from the pages of *House Beautiful* magazine. But if it's impossible to tell what color the front of your microwave oven is supposed to be and there's an inch of dust on top of your entertainment center (and you're too lazy to clean your house thoroughly before every ritual, class, workshop, or a coven member dropping by in a state of emergency), you're not ready to lead the group.

With a small child and multiple pets, including a hundred-pound long-haired dog that blows his coat (sheds all the undercoat at once) twice a year, my husband and I really had our work cut out for us when we decided to start a coven a few years ago. Left to our own devices, we're pretty messy people, so we were actually grateful for the full roster of classes, Sabbats, and moon rituals, because it made us keep the house reasonably clean at all times. I'm not saying it was easy, though.

Do I have my own act together?

Ideally, you should be in a reasonably stable stage in your life—done with school (including graduate school); comfortably pursuing a career or in a steady job that offers enough financial compensation to at least pay the bills; and either in a supportive, long-term emotional relationship or comfortable with your lack of one. Running a coven takes a lot of time: you have to interview every potential member, mediate and resolve conflicts between members, plan and execute at least eight holiday rituals and up to twenty-six moon rituals (assuming your group observes each new and full moon), plan and teach classes, and, as previously mentioned, have at least one shoulder available at all times for your fellow coven members to cry upon as needed. If a large percentage of your spare time is spent doing homework, worrying about money, trying to find a job, or cruising dating websites, you won't have time to lead your coven.

Are there other obligations in my life that need me more?

Aside from the time obligations, I'm talking about small children, non-Pagan significant others, and pets. Little kids take a lot of time, and (I say this from experience) once they reach the age of two until they're in high school, you're not likely to include them in ritual without excluding the needs of your other coven members. A little kid in ritual with all the sharp shiny things and open flame is going to command a lot of High Priestess Mom's and/or High Priest Dad's attention just so Toddler won't hurt himself. With that going on, how are you going to also monitor your first-time-in-ritual student who is about to make herself sick because she can't ground and center properly and you're too busy keeping Toddler's hand out of the candle to help her? Can you really find a 100 percent reliable babysitter for each and every ritual?

And, as I mentioned in chapter 2, in the section on basic Pagan etiquette, what if you have a potential student who is deathly afraid of, or violently allergic to, your long-haired dog? Do you have the strength to steer the student elsewhere because of your pre-existing commitment to your pet, knowing full well that in your town there may be no "elsewhere" to steer her to? What if you start the group and then your non-Pagan significant other tells you, "It's the group or me. Pick one." Consider your answer to these questions very carefully before you hang out your "I want to run a coven" shingle.

When my husband and I were first starting out in the coven-running business, we were also a foster home for a local no-kill animal shelter, so in addition to our own multiple pets, we usually had one or two extra dogs in the home that we were training to behave in a family environment to make them more adoptable. There were several times when, much as it pained me, I had to say, "Can I take Zoe/Lucky/

Tina next week? I'm having company this weekend." In other words, I didn't want to deal with a new good-natured-but-house-clueless dog and a living room full of coveners and guests for a Sabbat at the same time. It was hard, because dog rescue is as spiritual an activity to me as hosting ritual, but I had to find balance . . . until the time a litter of nine beagle puppies were born in my laundry room twenty-four hours before our Ostara ritual. All I can say is, it's a good thing baby animals are an appropriate spring motif!

How good are you at saying no?

I've done it—all good coven leaders have done it—taken on a member we shouldn't have, and suffered the consequences as teachers because of it. My least favorite ex-covener stole my husband's wedding ring that he'd taken off because it'd become too loose due to recent weight loss. Our "guts" told us not to accept him as a member, but we did anyway—mostly because he was friends with another of our members who begged us to take him in. Can you look a potential member in the eye and say, "No, you can't join"? What if she cries? Can you look a current member in the eye and say, "You need to leave"? What if he becomes angry? Again, consider these questions—and your answers—very carefully.

We once had to ask a student to leave the group because she could not—would not—forgive another student (and the first student's former best friend) for something. But we got to the point where our attempts at mediation broke down, the glowers across sacred space got to be too disruptive, and we said, "Enough." The sobs when we told the student to leave haunted us for a long time. It would have been easier to keep the one we asked to leave, but the second student showed more remorse and grew more as a person from the whole incident, so she's the one we asked to stay. It was one of the hardest things we ever had to do as coven leaders. I can say, "I hope I never have to do anything like that again," but realistically, if I'm running a coven, I know eventually I will have to.

Are you willing to lead a more than exemplary life?

This is probably the hardest part of being a coven leader—the constant spot on the Top Ten Gossip Topics list in your community. No matter how small or spread out your local Pagan community is, word will get around. And it doesn't matter what you do: if you are dating (serially or all at once) more than one person, you're a slut. If you're in a closed, monogamous relationship, you're a stuck-up prude. Every conflict you have with a member that results in the member leaving your coven will be blown all out of proportion by the local (and, thanks to the Internet, the not-so-local) Pagan community. You will be vilified, stabbed in the back, put on a pedestal, and worshipped—sometimes all by the same person at different times in your relationship, and always with the eyes of your fellow local Pagans upon you every step of the way. Can you live in a fishbowl? Because the minute you start to lead a training coven, you're new address is First Glass Container on the Right.

Back when A.G. and I were just friends, I once went out on a Friday-night date with a very nice man that unexpectedly turned into an overnighter. The coven I was running at the time had scheduled our Litha celebration for the next day, so I was very careful to get home in plenty of time to clean the house, prepare the ritual space, and make sure my contribution to the post-circle potluck was ready. In other words, I completely fulfilled my obligations to my group, even though I had been out all night. Unfortunately, my working partner had tried to reach me the evening before to discuss some ritual detail. This was in the time before cell phones, so of course I missed her call—and she'd called pretty late. When she arrived the next day for the ritual and found out where I'd been—and inferred correctly what I'd been doing—she said, "Gee, Bronwen, you really *are* a slut." Ouch. We didn't stay working partners for too long after that. And of course she thoroughly enjoyed spreading the story as far and wide as she could. I could say that her reaction to my personal life and the fact that she chose to tell the world in as nasty a way as possible didn't hurt—but I'd be lying.

This is not to say that leading a coven—even an informal, non-training coven—is not worth the trouble. Far from it. There is always the moment when you see the "Aha!" moment in a member's eyes as he gets, really gets, what the Gods are trying to tell him in ritual. That moment is the best reward there is. If you crave those moments, welcome to the few, the proud, the coven leaders!

The Survey Respondents' Perspective

I am currently considering joining a group. As in any other social situation, you get out of it what

you put in. I have taken time to build friendships.
The people in this group are slow to accept you
until you hang around and let them get to know
you. I think it's worth the time, but others complain
and say that they are snobs.

—K, SEVIERVILLE, TENNESSEE

Again, starting or joining a group is not that easy, as the survey respondents can attest. Some had good advice, and some had tales of caution and woe about their experiences of starting a coven. K makes a very good point—very often people in a formal group are perceived as "snobs" who think they're "better than" the solitaries in the area. The group members may not feel that way about themselves at all, but sometimes not only does the coven leader have to lead an exemplary, perfect, overly scrutinized life, but the rest of the coven does, too.

I have never tried to start a coven or other Pagan
group, but a friend did and it turned out to be a
disaster. It was hard for us to get together because
of conflicting work schedules. It also wasn't well-
organized, so nothing really "got done" when we
did get together, and one of the members brought
in several ex-girlfriends and it turned into a lot
of catfights and bickering, so we disbanded. In
another group I was involved with years ago, the
leader told us to always think twice about who we
invited because you never know how much dislike

and complications you can bring into a group by inviting the wrong person. That was really good advice, and I wish my friend had considered her choices more thoroughly instead of opening up to anyone who wanted to join us.

—KELTASIA, SHAMOKIN, PENNSYLVANIA

I am not really interested, at this time of my life, in organizing large groups, dealing with acting-out adolescents who want to shock their parents, or anyone who is more into being "out there" or in people's faces about their religious beliefs. I am also not willing to have people with serious mental illness or personality disorders in my personal circle. I certainly support everyone's right to deal with their spirituality in their own way, but I don't want to necessarily be a part of it. As a friend of mine once said: not everyone needs (or wants) to be a part of everything Pagan.

A common pitfall for me is getting too excited about the new Pagan I meet and wanting to include her or him before getting the "big picture" about this person.

—ROWEN BRIANNA, BOWLING GREEN, KENTUCKY

Rowen Brianna's comments about people with mental or personality issues may sound harsh, but chances are excellent that you are simply not trained to effectively work with such folks, no matter how much they may need what you and your group have to offer. One of my favorite sayings as a coven leader is "Religion is not a substitute for therapy." What I mean by this is that your coven, your rituals, and your classes are not a good or effective alternative for someone who genuinely needs professional help, no matter how much they (and you) want your events and the training you're giving to be an effective alternative. It's amazing how quickly a person who needs professional help can monopolize your rituals, your classes, and the rest of your coven life.

A.G. and I once had a student who was bright, funny, articulate, dedicated—and probably the most insecure person we had ever met. She absolutely, positively had to be the center of attention at all coven rituals, classes, and social get-togethers. If she wasn't the center of attention, she always had a crisis that restored her to the role of primary group focus—she had to leave her (allegedly) abusive boyfriend *right now*; she was being "forced" to draw down her chosen deity; the deity was then asking her to do awful things. The list went on and on. Finally, exhausted, A.G. and I realized we'd made a huge mistake and asked her to leave until she was in a better space to do the work the coven was formed to do. Funny, she never came back.

A wise coven leader will know when someone needs more help than the leader can effectively offer, and will set firm boundaries by not allowing the person to join the group—or asking him or her to leave if already a member—until the person has received the needed help.

Pagan author Amber K has written an excellent, comprehensive book on starting and running a coven.[17] I highly recommend it.

For the Truly Brave: Public Events

Whether your little band of intrepid small-town Pagans chooses to stay a small discussion group or morphs into a coven, eventually the topic of "going public" is bound to come up. The more comfortable your group feels about its existence, the greater the temptation to try a Pagan Pride picnic or even a public ritual. Here are some tips for a successful public event:

Mask it as something else

The Pagans in my husband's hometown of Salina, Kansas, decided to have a Pagan Pride picnic a few years ago. They very cleverly scheduled it near the end of the Pagan Pride season in mid-October and said very specifically in all of the publicity that everyone attending should dress up in costume, especially children. That way if any non-Pagans came by and asked what they were doing, they could answer (more or less honestly), "We're having an early Halloween party." Just a few years before this picnic, a non-Pagan health food store in town was actively shut down (as opposed to "went out of business"), so the Salina Pagans were pretty brave to meet in public at all.

---

17. Amber K, *Coven Craft: Witchcraft for Three or More* (Llewellyn, 2002).

While it's hard to pretend a ritual is anything other than a ritual, a Pagan Pride picnic could be a "medieval re-enactor's event," a "Going Green festival," or, as in Salina, Kansas, a "Halloween party."

Take it out of town

Your picnic or ritual does not need to be in the park right next to the elementary school. Find a county park or state park nearby with picnic tables, a shelter, Porta-Johns, and a couple of permanent barbecue grills—and you are all set. The rangers probably won't ask why you want to rent the space, and you don't have to volunteer the information. However, you will need to adhere to park rules regarding weapons (athames and swords may qualify; check your state statutes), alcohol, pets, noise ordinances (which may prohibit drumming if there are residences nearby), and fires in places other than the grills provided. *Make absolutely sure you have your space permit paperwork with you at the event.* Be good stewards of the earth; even if there are trash cans onsite, plan to take your full garbage bags away with you. Pick up previous users' trash while you're there.

Appoint a media spokesperson in advance

If you are in town and doing something interesting, there is a chance someone from the local paper could show up. As a journalist, I can tell you from experience that small-town newspaper reporters have a sixth sense about these things. As part of your planning, decide who will be the person to talk to the press—if they come—and help your new media spokesperson come up with a list of possible questions and calm, rational, well-thought-out answers.

Have fully charged cell phones available

Don't assume your fellow organizers will have their cell phones on them "because they always do." You never know when someone will get hurt and need an ambulance, a child might get lost, or, Gods forbid, you need to call the police because a passerby has major issues with you being in public or your pesky local reporter just won't go away. Discuss in advance who should call the authorities—and under what circumstances.

Keep it short

If there's a ritual, half an hour to forty-five minutes in circle *maximum* is good. The entire event does not need to last all day. Three to four hours for a quick ritual and potluck meal is good, and will give attendees a long window of arrival and departure times.

Adopt a charity

Plan to make a charity part of your event. Have participants bring cans of food that you can later donate to the nearest food bank—you can use the group's name or not. Ask participants to bring cans of pet food or boxes of kitty litter for the local animal shelter, or paper, notebooks, and pens for the local school-supply drive.

I will freely admit that large public ritual is not my area of expertise. Isaac Bonewits, however, wrote an excellent book on the subject.[18]

When Alone Is Better

This is not to say that you must interact with other Pagans; there are certainly advantages to staying solitary and never meeting a fellow spiritual traveler.

One good reason to stay solitary is the prior family and pets commitment I've mentioned. Also, if you have a special-needs child and the financial and personal-care logistics of actually attending even a local Pagan event is too much, you should not feel guilty for keeping your practice private. If you have too much to do at home, don't go.

There is a certain amount of positive self-reliance that one can feel by staying solitary. No one else is responsible for your spiritual development but you; if you want to grow and improve, it's completely up to you and the Gods how you will do so.

And if you've met the other Pagans in the area and you just don't feel comfortable interacting with them, then by all means don't—your "gut" may be telling you something about your mental health or physical safety. Listen to it.

But for the rest of you who crave and want to work toward a connection to local Pagans, I can only say: If you build it, they will come. I truly believe this.

---

18. Isaac Bonewits, *Neopagan Rites: A Guide to Creating Public Rituals That Work* (Llewellyn, 2007).

CHAPTER 8

Problems, Like Charity, Begin at Home

I've never had any real issues regarding my faith in the workplace, probably because I kept it low-key. I was working in a nursing home and could speak to any of our patients about death/dying/religious issues openly without specifically stating what my religion was, because they wanted help with reconciling what they were going through with their own religion.

—KELTASIA, SHAMOKIN, PENNSYLVANIA

Overall, the survey respondents said, and I agree, that the two hardest things about being a small-town Pagan are how your path will be perceived by co-workers and supervisors, and whether or not to raise your children openly Pagan. Emigrants may be used to a certain degree of acceptance, tolerance, or just plain apathy—no one at work gives a damn what you call yourself just so you get to the office on time and do your job while you're there. Emigrant children may be accustomed to more culturally diverse classrooms/classmates and music teachers who stay away from Christmas carols completely.

Hometowners, on the other hand, may have the added burden of bosses and co-workers who have known them their whole lives, and who might notice and comment when they don't show up at church anymore. Their children may be the second or third (or more) generation to attend the local school and may have some of the same teachers as their now-Pagan parents, which can lead to some pretty awkward parent-teacher conferences.

Not surprisingly, single Emigrants who have moved to a small town because of their career and single Hometowners reported some difficulty finding a partner, but each survey respondent was very firm on one romantic issue: it's far better to stay single than to be in a relationship with someone who doesn't share, or at least tolerate, your Pagan path.

Problems on the Job

When my husband and I lived in Columbia, Missouri, we were pretty well-known within the Pagan community. We ran a training coven, we participated in (and often led) the monthly Pagan Night Out, and we occasionally acted as High Priest and High Priestess for public Sabbats. Because of this, and because some of our students were also in college, we could count on giving at least two interviews apiece per semester, either for the University of Missouri student newspaper or as the subject of a paper in a women's studies or comparative religion class.

We also occasionally participated in panel discussions on topics like the origin of Halloween, or contemporary Paganism versus anthropological and historical perspectives (it was a university town, after all), that were covered by the local newspaper, the *Columbia Daily Tribune*. In other words, my husband's professors, PhD committee, and fellow graduate students, and the upper management at my insurance-company job, had ample opportunities to read in some media format or other that we were Pagan. I don't know if they did or not; neither of us experienced any repercussions at our respective jobs.

In the fall of 2005 I was working in the admissions office of Eastern New Mexico University in Portales, New Mexico, where my husband was a professor. As I mentioned earlier, there had been a Pagan student group on campus, and some of the members wanted to get it started again. I volunteered to let the weekly student newspaper interview me for the Halloween issue. Maybe some Pagan or at least Pagan-curious students would read the piece and express interest in jump-starting the Pagan student group. It was a good article, very fair, and the student reporter worked hard to quote me properly (as a former journalism major myself, I appreciate this sort of thing even more). No one in my "chain of command" at work said anything to me, including the vice-president of admissions.

However, and maybe it was just a coincidence, but from the day my "interview a Witch for Halloween" article came out, my immediate supervisor began to make my life a living hell. Oh, nothing that could be proven, and nothing big—it was little things like pointing out my errors in as loud a voice as possible, checking to see how I was doing with my stack of work twice as often (at least) as she checked with anyone else, allowing other employees to arrive a few minutes late and leave a few minutes early without recrimination (but I had to stay until five o'clock sharp to cover the phones all the time), and treating me in a condescending way that just set my teeth on edge.

I complained and was told to "suck it up," that it was "just your imagination." The situation eventually got to the point that I would burst into tears every morning at the thought of having to go to work. That's when my husband jeopardized his own professor career and confronted my supervisor's boss about it. She called me into her office after he left and laughed, saying how "cute he was" to stand up for me. Since he slammed her office door so hard I heard it from half a building away when he arrived, I still sometimes wonder about her definition of "cute."

Eventually, it was made clear to me that I was in a position where I could either quit my job or get fired, so I quit. Was the newspaper article responsible for my slow descent into the job from hell? I will never know for sure. But I will also think twice and evaluate my work environment very carefully before I allow myself to be interviewed by non-Pagan media again.

Many of the survey respondents echo this sentiment, and choose not to be "out" as Pagans, or are only "out" to a few select people, at work:

> *It has made the workplace a little "sticky" at times, but all in all I tell them, "Don't be friends with me because of my beliefs, but instead be my friend because of who I am." That works pretty well, actually.*
>
> *It also helped that one of my boss's daughters went through a year and a day of study with me. At first I had conflicts with our mechanic, as I was a school bus driver. He is very Christian, but over time he learned that I wasn't going to sacrifice any kid or anything, and he became one of my closest friends. He and I learned to respect each others' beliefs even if we didn't agree with them.*
>
> —JENN, MOUNTAIN HOME, IDAHO

> *I will probably come out gradually as people know me*
> *as a person and as a professional . . . or not. It de-*
> *pends on the climate and who really needs to know. I*
> *don't enjoy other people's religious diatribes, and not*
> *participating in that discussion at work is a way to*
> *do that. I generally say, "My spiritual path doesn't*
> *lend itself to organized religion and is personal. Why*
> *is it important for you to know?" The last sentence is*
> *reserved for the truly nosy and annoying.*
>
> —ROWEN BRIANNA, BOWLING GREEN, KENTUCKY

> *I lost a job once because the boss found out I took*
> *a workshop at the local New Age shop. Stupidly,*
> *the shop confirmed I had been there and explained*
> *what was discussed to my boss. Worse yet, it was a*
> *horrible workshop.*
>
> —NOEY, COUPEVILLE, WASHINGTON

Surprisingly, other respondents reported no work problems at all. I can honestly say I've had jobs in addition to
the insurance-company job where it wasn't an issue. In fact,
this past St. Patrick's Day my workplace had some information about the origins of the holiday and other information
about Ireland. I had to smile when I saw the poster on St.
Brigid that started "St. Brigid was originally a Celtic goddess . . ." I openly wear pentacle earrings every day at this
job, and not one person has noticed—or at least noticed
enough to say anything. On the other hand, I do work in
a medium-sized town where crazy Pagans can wear satin,

thigh-length leopard-print bathrobes to Walmart and no one says anything. Whether or not to be "out" on the job, and the possible ramifications, truly need to be evaluated on a case-by-case basis.

> *My bosses have been understanding, and have let me have time off when I needed it.*
>
> —EVY, BOLIVAR, NEW YORK

> *I've had no negative experiences. At my husband's workplace (in Madison), everyone knows what I believe, and I have not had anything but questions and positive reinforcement.*
>
> —WITCH OF THE WOODS, MERRIMAC, WISCONSIN

Raising Your Children Pagan

We've all heard the horror stories of raising Pagan children in small-town America—everything from the kids being suspended from school for wearing a pentacle to child and family service agencies removing children from the home simply because the parents are Pagan. Frankly, I expected that at least some of my survey respondents would have heartbreaking tales to tell about losing (or almost losing) their kids, major harassment at school, or something equally horrible. But, as you will see by the comments in this section, they didn't. As a trained journalist, I can only report the stories I get or find and can confirm; I didn't receive any hair-raising stories about raising Pagan children in small-town America, so I can't report any here.

That doesn't mean the stories we do hear haven't happened, but bear in mind that we don't know all the details of those cases. In general, my survey respondents said—and I completely agree—that if you want to stay off the radar of child protective services because you're raising your kids Pagan, make sure the interior and exterior of your home is reasonably clean; your children eat breakfast before they go to school every morning (or make arrangements for them to eat at school); they don't wear the same dirty clothes to class every day (unless they're teenagers and that's the new "thing"); and make sure they're healthy and do their homework every night. Once the authorities see one of the "red flags" (unhealthily filthy home, hungry or dirty child, etc.), you've basically given them an excuse to investigate you thoroughly, whether you live in a small town or not.

That being said, many parents in the survey were happy to share their Pagan parenting experiences.

> *My daughter knows about the Goddess and the God and about stones and the Great Spirit and a lot of other things. She also knows the elements and other things, too. When she was born, her father asked me to make sure to teach the Pagan way, as he knew he wouldn't be around to teach her. He is still fine with it today.*

*She is still my pride and joy, and she is a walker
of the light. She is now ten and I couldn't be prouder.*
—JENN, MOUNTAIN HOME, IDAHO

There are many thorough and comprehensive books on rais-ing your children Pagan, including my favorite—Pagan par-ent, author, and teacher Kristin Madden's excellent *Pagan Parenting*,[19] so I will not go into too much detail here. I met Kristin and her family at a small Pagan gathering a couple of years ago, and her son is a great model of the Pagan child I want to raise—grounded, gentle, knowledgeable, polite, and still interested in normal teenage-appropriate activities. In short, he's everything a parent (Pagan or not) could ask for.

My husband and I are raising our daughter Pagan. When she was a toddler, she quickly learned to blow kisses at the full moon; now that she's a little older, she blows kisses to the moon no matter what phase it's in! Like any preschooler, she is enthusiastic about holiday activities such as trick-or-treating, decorating a Christmas/Yule tree, and coloring (and finding) Easter eggs. My daughter even made homemade butter with us last Imbolc. Rose is also the one who blesses the food at suppertime, and we say the following prayer at bedtime every night:

Lord and Lady, keep me safe all night

And guard my family 'til morning light.

---

19. *Pagan Parenting: Spiritual, Magical & Emotional Development of the Child* (Spilled Candy Publications, 2004).

She then gets to list all the family members, including the dogs, and ends with "So be it." It's going to break my heart when she decides she's too old to say prayers with Mommy anymore. In the meantime, Rose loves to sit in ritual and will probably be better at reading tarot cards than I am by the time she's out of elementary school. She comes by that talent naturally, though. Her father is an accomplished reader, and my mother-in-law is the first person I ever saw who read with an ordinary deck of playing cards. She was scarily accurate, too!

Many of the survey respondents are also choosing to raise their children Pagan or Pagan-friendly. Even those in relationships in which their significant other isn't Pagan, or who have stepchildren whose other parent is Christian, somehow convey a little of our path to the kids in the home.

> *My boys have attended church services with their dad and circles with me. I am trying to show them both types of religion and practices, so they will be better informed of their choices as they get older.*
>
> —KELTASIA, SHAMOKIN, PENNSYLVANIA

> *I am [raising my daughter Pagan], but I'm also teaching [her] other religions and letting her choose her own path. I will not force what I believe on anyone.*
>
> —SPIRITRUNNER, BAKERSFIELD, CALIFORNIA
> (FORMERLY IN TAFT, CALIFORNIA)

> *My stepchildren understand our ways are different*
> *from their mother's. We're not raising them totally*
> *Pagan, but they are learning our ways.*
>
> —DEANNA EBERLIN, ADDISON, NEW YORK

Other parents have decided not to raise their children Pagan. The interesting thing is, the parents who choose this course of action did not necessarily base their decisions on the fact that they live in a small town, but on more personal considerations:

> *I'm not raising my son specifically Pagan, no. My*
> *husband and I have come to the conclusion that it is*
> *possible to teach morals and values outside of any*
> *religious framework.*
>
> —BECCA, CLOVIS, NEW MEXICO

> *I did not raise my children Pagan as such, but did*
> *teach them to respect Mother Earth and honor the*
> *seasonal cycle.*
>
> —DONNA HAMES, NASHWAUK, MINNESOTA

One thing to keep in mind, especially in a small town, whether you consciously decide to raise your child Pagan or let him discover Paganism on his own: kids are the cruelest people on the planet. Sometimes deliberately, sometimes by accident, but wounds (even verbal wounds) inflicted on the playground or in the classroom can remain unhealed well into adulthood. Think about this very carefully before your child starts school. As of this writing, my daughter will start kindergarten in about two months. I know I worry about how my choice to raise her Pagan will affect her.

> *There isn't enough space in this book to describe all the negativity I was on the receiving end of when I was still in school. Gods alive, that was hideous. I used to wear this chunky pentacle that I picked up at Spencer's, silver with blue stones at the points. They were a dime a dozen, and I think every kid who considered themselves Pagan that went through my school had one at one point. Anyway, people would see it and treat me like a leper, call me names, cross themselves as I went by.*
>
> *School life was hell. I was constantly harassed; I was bullied; I was pulled into the office and basically told I was on the school's "watchlist" of potentially dangerous students because I was the target of hostility. The Columbine massacre had happened my junior year, just before prom, so of course every school went into hyper-paranoia about who was going to be next, and because I was the little goth weirdo who was allegedly into Satanism, I was pegged to be a potential threat. The administration never bothered to actually get to know me or anything. They heard what people said about me; they saw me being bullied; and I guess it didn't take much effort to imagine me coming to school with guns concealed upon my person.*
>
> —RAVENNA, DOWAGIAC, MICHIGAN

In school I was ridiculed, picked on, and persecuted.
I even had people go as far as throwing holy water
on me and throwing frozen water bottles at me in
the outside eating area. Of course the school dis-
trict, the principal, and superintendent would do
nothing to stop it because it was their "star" foot-
ball players who were harassing me.

—SPIRITRUNNER, BAKERSFIELD, CALIFORNIA
(FORMERLY IN TAFT, CALIFORNIA)

Some parents choose to take a proactive approach and discuss the basics of their Pagan faith with teachers or other
school administrators. A friend of ours in Missouri did this
from the time his daughter entered kindergarten. She is now
about to graduate from high school and, as far as I know, has
never had any trouble with her Paganism in school.

On the other hand, my mother, who taught music in the
elementary school in our town for a couple of decades, coun-
sels against telling the teachers. Her opinion is that unless
you believe your child will not or should not participate in
a particular school activity because of his religion, you don't
need to "rock the boat" and say anything to the teachers. Apparently, many of her students over the years were Jehovah's
Witnesses. The parents asked that their children not sing
any holiday or patriotic songs. My mother complied, and
that was the end of the issue. So unless your school's music
teacher is asking the kids to sing Christmas hymns in December, maybe it's just better to keep your child's religion quiet.
On the other hand, we may teach our daughter to say "one

nation under Gods" during the Pledge of Allegiance—A. G. and I are still talking about this issue, and may just table it until she's old enough for "under God" to bother her.

Sometimes it's the teacher's religion and not yours that can cause a problem. A few years ago, my non-religious nephew in Salina, Kansas, and his classmates were all being pressured by his second-grade teacher to either join her church or go to Hell. Nice situation for a seven-year-old, no? My mother-in-law took offense and stormed down to the school. According to my husband, she marched into the classroom, grabbed the offending teacher by the ear (ow!), and dragged her to the principal's office. Much yelling on my mother-in-law's part ensued, the gist of which was "This is not appropriate in the classroom. Do something." What she actually said is not allowed in a book like this that minors might read. The principal agreed and the teacher, amazingly, stopped proselytizing, at least to her students.

> *I've had to argue with the school board about their enforced prayer and "God issues." I do occasionally wear my pentacle to school functions. Since quite a few of the parents already knew me before my conversion, it hasn't made a difference to them. But it does seem to bother the administration—even though my kids get As and Bs regularly and have not had any real disciplinary problems.*
>
> —KELTASIA, SHAMOKIN, PENNSYLVANIA

When our eldest began kindergarten, we had a discussion with her teacher about seasonal holidays and were pleased to learn that she decorated for all of them. A few years later, we had similar discussions with the younger two children's teachers and school administrators. We explained to them that we are Pagan, and there would be no tolerance of questioning our children's beliefs on the subject. There weren't any problems.

—MOONDANCER, WASHINGTON STATE

Fitting in on Sunday Morning

One of the biggest social discrepancies between children who are being raised Pagan and their friends who live in actively Christian homes is the question of what the kids do on Sunday morning. The Christian kids, obviously, go to Sunday school and church while the Pagan kids don't. Emigrant children may come to a small town thinking this difference is no big deal. Hometowner kids probably know better.

When we lived in Portales, New Mexico, my husband and I briefly attended the local Unitarian Fellowship for the first six months or so of our daughter's life. In fact, she is still listed on the registry somewhere; our daughter is officially a Unitarian, but we are not! There's an old Unitarian joke: "What do you call an atheist with kids? A Unitarian." This was certainly true in our Fellowship, but after a few months we got tired of sitting around and talking about religion on Sunday morning rather than actually practicing it, so we stopped going.[20]

One survey question was "Are you and your family attending church regularly or semi-regularly as a 'cover'? If so, which one?" Most survey respondents, again, said either no, or *hell* no.

> *I do not attend church to put on an appearance of something I'm not. If people don't like it, that's their problem, not mine. When asked about it, I just explain that I don't have to be in a specific building to communicate with my Creator.*
>
> —KELTASIA, SHAMOKIN, PENNSYLVANIA

> *If I want a "church," I'll walk outside to my garden or meditation pond.*
>
> —SPIRITRUNNER, BAKERSFIELD, CALIFORNIA
> (FORMERLY IN TAFT, CALIFORNIA)

I *love* Spiritrunner's answer, don't you?

Children at Pagan Gatherings

Pretty much every kid I've ever seen at a Pagan festival looked very happy to be there. I've seen children who started coming to gatherings at a young age, and they are the happiest, most self-confident kids I know. If it's a big deal for adults

---

20. I know that many, if not most, Unitarian Fellowships are more celebratory and less cerebral; this was just an odd group.

who live in small towns to discover that they're not alone and there's this all-Pagan space that they can revel in for the next four or five days, imagine how much that same environment would mean to a child. Not only will Mom and Dad recharge their spiritual batteries by connecting with their "tribe," but so will the kids. At almost every Pagan gathering I've attended or been in charge of, the ones not old enough to be interested in the workshops are almost never found on their own—they tend to travel in big, multi-aged "packs."

Now here's the problem: as great as a gathering is for kids, not only will they likely see adults who aren't their parents in various stages of undress, but the children themselves may also want to wear much less than they normally would at home.

This is a big issue, not just for Pagan parents but for the entire community. In general, people who do not want to circle with kids (little ones in particular) can create or find an adults-only group. In a small town, however, this could become a problem if there's only one group and it's not the kind you need, either child-friendly or determinedly child-free, but with a little determination and a few extra miles on your car, you can keep your ritual time exactly as you like it—anything from kid-inclusive to skyclad-adults-only.

But people mingle at a Pagan gathering, whether it's in the vendor area, at the nightly concert, in main ritual, or even on the way to the communal shower. Sure, you can do your best to keep your children in the "clothing-mandatory family camping area" that many festivals provide, but what if they want to go shopping on Merchant's Row? Or go swimming in the camp pond or swimming pool? Or eat lunch in the dining hall?

I wish I could give definitive advice on this issue, but as a parent and as a former festival coordinator, I can't. Nor can my survey respondents. Every gathering is different, every family is different, and every family's stance on children seeing nude adults and strangers seeing their children nude or semi-nude is different.

Even within the same family, opinions can differ. My husband is adamant that Rose not attend a Pagan gathering that is clothing optional until she's in her mid-thirties (which is roughly the age he'd prefer she be when she starts seriously dating). I agree she's not quite ready to accompany me to various gatherings—she's going through an "afraid of the dark" phase that's not conducive to tent camping, and at five she's not old enough to hang out at the kid's activity area without me, and I'm usually pretty busy vending and/or teaching workshops. However, I am completely convinced that if we treat the naked human body as no big deal, Rose will too. Needless to say, discussion will probably continue on this issue for some time.

Whichever stance you take, you *must* check the state statutes for not only your home state but the state in which the gathering takes place. Missouri, for instance, has very strict laws about adults "exposing themselves" to minors—which could include the scenario of a skyclad adult standing next to a sixteen-year-old (or a five-year-old) at a merchant's booth or even rinsing off under the next spray in a communal shower house. If you live in one of the stricter states, legally speaking, and your kid goes home after a gathering and starts talking about all the naked grown-ups he or she saw, you could be in big trouble. And if the state in question has even stricter laws about adults *and* minors being minus a few critical items of clothing in each others' presence, you could find yourself in need of a Pagan-friendly lawyer very quickly.

Relationship Issues

As I mentioned, one of the toughest issues facing a small-town Pagan is his or her non-relationship status. In a large city, it's much easier to find a mate of like mind and compatible beliefs, but in a small town, where it's hard enough to collect a group of people to get together and even *talk* about Paganism, meeting your life partner is often far less likely—and a lot more work.

Again, I expected the survey respondents to send me at least a handful of horror stories about relationships that had either never gotten off the ground or broken up over the issue of one party's Pagan practice—acrimonious divorce, loud public breakups, something—and I didn't get any. I know there are marriages and long-term relationships that have crumbled the minute one of the couple said the "P" word, including my first marriage, but no one who volunteered to talk to me had anything to say on this issue. Again, as a journalist, I can only report on the stories I get and can then verify.

I can certainly say with some authority that finding a Pagan or at least Pagan-friendly life partner is of utmost importance whether you're a Hometowner or an Emigrant.

Julia, of East Stroudsburg, Pennsylvania, hit the nail on the head when she said, "When I was dating after my divorce, I chose to only date people who were at least open to Paganism. I was looking for someone to share my entire life with, including my religion."

As I mentioned, my first husband was/is a born-again Christian who is now a happy Episcopalian. We were both (nominally on my part) Christian when we married, and my exploring Paganism is what broke up the marriage.

My second husband, although Pagan, was an alcoholic, a drug abuser, and a wife abuser. At one point I found myself facing the business end of a loaded gun, and he was threatening to pull the trigger. Why? He was initiated, I was not,[21] and I'd just had the bad manners to say I knew more about something Pagan-related than he did. The lesson here is obvious: just because someone is also Pagan does not mean that you should automatically think he or she is a nice person who will make good lifemate material.

My third husband, A.G., who is also the father of my daughter and the one I left the big city of Washington, DC for, is not only Pagan, but he was so when I met him. Over time, our paths have merged and we are magical working partners in addition to being spouses, co-parents, and best friends. But just because our paths have merged doesn't mean we share every single spiritual aspect of our lives. He grows organic vegetables as a form of spiritual expression; I have a

---

21. And, boy, do I have a few choice things to say to the person(s) who thought he was appropriate initiate material.

black thumb. I sing as a form of spiritual expression; he can't carry a tune in a bucket. His favorite altars are the stove and the kitchen counters. I worship my God best by walking my dog. But we have the same strong opinions about how rituals and ritual groups are to be run; we work with deities who are compatible with each other, and that is merged enough. Remember, every person's path is a little different.

In between these three husbands I dated a lot (and I mean a *lot*) of Pagan or Pagan-friendly men. Some I went out with only once, others I dated for years. And I lived in the Baltimore-Washington metropolitan area, where there was a sizeable community to pick from. I was living in Baldwin City, Kansas, when I first met A.G., and I live there now, so I'll turn to the experts on how to search for a life mate in a small town:

> *Being Pagan made it really tough because they never understood why I was doing things; it would piss them off when I was doing ritual or something and not with them.*
>
> —JENN, MOUNTAIN HOME, IDAHO

> *That's almost the last thing I worry about, and I worry about a lot of things. Does he think I'm homely? Does he think I'm fat? Oh Gods, is my voice really that annoying? What if I say something stupid and he tells all his friends about the dimwit he went out with last night? The Pagan thing rarely crosses my mind, but when I do think about it, I*

get really freaked out. I know so many people that see my faith as a quirk or just something else that's weird about me, something to just smile and nod about when I open my mouth. I get a bit worried that I'll meet my dream guy and have him end up treating my beliefs as "just another weird phase my kooky girlfriend is in." I would love to find a mate who's either Pagan or agnostic.

—RAVENNA, DOWAGIAC, MICHIGAN

Well, I'm not looking for a mate. Right now I'm enjoying my own self. However, if at any point I do want to look for a mate, he will have to be a practicing Pagan. I can't be in a relationship with someone whose religion wants to burn me at the stake.

—K, SEVIERVILLE, TENNESSEE

I'm bisexual. So it's hard to find anyone, period. In this conservative town, you have to go way outside the city limits before people are even remotely comfortable with telling you they're interested. And the funny thing is I know lots of gay men, but no gay women.

—EVY, BOLIVAR, NEW YORK

You're a WHAT? Telling a Non-Pagan Love Interest That You're Pagan

It can happen, despite your best efforts; you've fallen in love with someone in your small town and—lo and behold—he or she has not gotten the memo that you're Pagan. What do you do?

Here's one way: I was on a date one time with a non-Pagan, but he was a serious science fiction fan. I can't remember if it was the first date or the second one, when the guy said, "Oh, by the way, I'm a filker." A filker, in case you don't know, is someone who attends a lot (and I mean a *lot*) of science fiction conventions for the sole purpose of staying up until two or three in the morning singing songs with old, familiar tunes and new lyrics about *Star Trek*. Or whatever the latest science fiction or fantasy fandom craze may be.

To prove it, my date burst into song. Loudly. In the middle of the restaurant.

At least he had a nice voice.

Needless to say, the relationship didn't last too long after that. But did he do the right thing?

Actually, yes, he did. He came out and told me, which was brave of him. Not many people like filkers. So my first rule of thumb for dropping a "big surprise" like "I'm Pagan" on someone you're seeing is: you have to tell them.

My second rule of thumb, however, may surprise you: Don't tell them on the first date. Maybe not even on the second date. Why? Give him or her a chance to get to know you first, without the big neon sign flashing WEIRD! or SCARY! over your head. Let your potential sweetie start to like you for your positive, "ordinary" qualities—great sense of humor, nice smile, levelheaded in a crisis, even temperament—before letting him or her know that in a couple weeks you're going on vacation to a Pagan gathering two states away with about a thousand of your closest, clothing-optional friends.

So my third rule of thumb is: Don't wait too long. Because then you can add resentment to the possible reaction list, since "you kept it from me!"

Rule number four: When you do decide to tell him or her, don't drop hints or waffle and definitely don't act ashamed of who you are and what you believe. Explain your situation calmly and intelligently, but don't dump too much on your sweetie all at once. And don't expect instant acceptance or an instant conversion to your Pagan faith. Offer to give your new love some time to assimilate what you've said.

My rule number five: Leave him or her with a graceful way to exit from the relationship if he or she truly cannot handle what you've said. Yes, it will hurt like hell, but better some hurt now than a whole mess of hurt later, after you've had enough time to *really* invest your heart and soul into the relationship.

Finally, be hopeful! Your new sweetie might just surprise you and say, "Wow! I'm Pagan, too! I just never knew what it was called!"

Two Religions, One Relationship

Believe it or not, even if your significant other is not Pagan, you can make your relationship work as long as the other person is open-minded about your path. (I would not recommend dating a Baptist minister, for example.) Even if you are both Pagan, there may be some fundamental differences in your practice and teachings that can cause a rift. My friend David in Canada, for instance, is Wiccan and also dedicated to the African Orishas. Just because a lover or a roommate is Pagan doesn't mean that person knows the specifics of David's two religious practices, which can include strict dietary, hygiene, and wardrobe requirements.

How, then, can you share a home, share a bathroom, and share your free time, intimate bodily fluids, and a tub of popcorn at the movies, and not share a religion? The answers are much easier than you might think.

Read, Read, and Read Some More

The more you know about your sweetie's religious practices and ideals, the more you're likely to find they have a lot in common with your own, even if, for example, he's a Buddhist and you follow the old Norse warrior gods. Every religion strives to explain the Unexplainable, the Godhead if you wish. And many faiths have very similar paths that lead to the One.

Something to keep in mind, though: be very picky about *what* you read. If, for instance, your beloved is Catholic, *don't* confine your reading to works that make Catholics look, well, not so good—like stories about the Inquisition. Your partner's spiritual mentor (priest, rabbi, etc.) probably has an office filled with books by contemporary authors who discuss the religion in question in a spiritually honest yet academic way. Ask to borrow some of these books.

Try the Hands-On Approach

Go to your partner's place of worship at least once in a while (on Christmas Eve or during the Jewish high holidays, for example), especially if you want him or her to occasionally circle with you. Knowing what really happens during your mate's religious services has three huge advantages. One, you get to see your partner's religious ideals in action. Two, you'll make your sweetie very happy by your attendance. Three, if you ever need (for social or emotional support reasons) to accompany your partner to a rite of passage—i.e., a wedding or a funeral—you already have some idea of what to expect and how to behave.

I offer the following secular example: my husband was raised in a military family; his father was career Army. I was raised by two semi-hippie, war-protesting music teachers. We did not attend his father's funeral in 2003 due to issues with his family dynamics (see the story in chapter 1 about his sister calling us "freaks" in the intensive care unit), but, if we had, I would have been completely lost and confused by the military funeral. I would not have known how to behave or what was expected of me, and consequently would have been less able to provide A.G. with optimum support in a time of need.

So go to church with your partner. I'm not saying you have to stay afterward for the food and chit-chat, nor am I advocating participating in parts of the service you may feel uncomfortable about (like communion for us non-Christians), but at least try to attend the service with an open mind. You might find something of spiritual value to you. I'm honestly convinced I would have found the military aspects of my father-in-law's funeral to be quite lovely.

Incorporate Both Sets of Holidays into Your Home

This is particularly important if one or both of you have either brought children into the relationship, or you've had some of your own since you got together. If your sweetie is Jewish, for instance, be open to celebrating Hanukkah, Passover, or Yom Kippur along with Yule, Ostara, and Mabon. You may just find some similarities between the different religions' seasonal holidays that you didn't know existed before.

Even within differing Pagan traditions, there can be a lot of lovely crossover. When my husband and I got together, he told me that his family, German Lutherans all, celebrate St. Nicholas Day on December 6 by putting their shoes out the night before. St. Nicholas then comes and fills them. It's kind of like a barometer for Santa Claus at Christmas: if you're good, you get candy, fruit, or a small toy item. If you're not, then you get coals or sticks in your shoe. Celebrating St. Nicholas Day helps our daughter learn about her German heritage; it makes my husband happy; and yeah, okay, it's really fun! So put up a Yule tree, light the menorah, and relax!

Keep Your Negative Opinions to Yourself

No, you're not going to love everything about your partner's non-Pagan faith, and he or she probably doesn't love everything about yours. If you did, one of you would have converted by now, and you probably wouldn't be reading this section of the book. However, I cannot stress strongly enough that you should *not* express these opinions out loud to your sweetie, even if he or she asks! It would also be a good idea not to express them too strongly to your mutual friends—they may accidentally tell your partner. Look, as long as no one's pressuring you to convert, all is good. Leave it alone and chalk it up to just another difference between two people who love each other very much. My husband thinks good bratwurst is another face of the God. I can't stand the stuff. We manage.

Bronwen's Big Theory of Deity

Keep in mind that all religions are designed to bring the follower closer to the Divine as they see it, and, as such, they all have value. To illustrate this, I'm going to share with you Bronwen's Big Theory of Deity. As I do, please bear in mind that I am a huge fan of Big Band music and that I came of age when disco was king.

The Supreme Power of the Universe, by whatever name you call Him or Her, is like a giant mirror ball, reflecting Light down upon us all. Now, the human brain is just not equipped to comprehend the incredible vastness and power of the whole Mirror Ball. So I'm standing over here on this side of the Grand Mirror Ball, and that little square there is shining Light onto my face. I really like that little square. I can relate to it. However, you're over on the other side of the Grand Mirror Ball (it's not spinning at the moment, okay?), and a completely different little square is shining Light on you. And you like your little square as much as I like mine. Yes, the squares are different, meaning the name of (the) God(s), styles and methods of worship, and philosophies about the True Nature of Life are different. But, and here's the important part: *They're both part of the same mirror ball!*

Cool, huh?

——— CHAPTER 9 ———

The Experts Speak

The last question on my survey was "What would you like to tell me about life as a small-town Pagan that has not been covered?" You've gotten my answer to this question in bits and pieces throughout the book. This is what the respondents, my experts, wanted to leave you with. There's an awful lot of wisdom here:

> *There are a lot of people out there who want to know [about Paganism] and don't know where to go, so just be yourself and they will come to you. There are also a lot of Pagan wannabes out there*

who do things to give us a bad name, so be careful who you get involved with. Look at their personal relationships and you will know if they are empowered individuals or not.

—JENN, MOUNTAIN HOME, IDAHO

Being a Pagan in a small town is no more difficult (or any less so) than it is in a city. Well, maybe slightly easier—I can walk outside and be "lost in nature" in less than one minute or however long it takes me to walk to the back of our property. There's less noise and light pollution here, and you tend to be a bit more aware of nature and its rhythm and cycles than you do in a city. That may seem somewhat idealized, but it's true.

—MOONDANCER, WASHINGTON STATE

I grew up Catholic, which didn't do much for me. I found Wicca first when I was seventeen; I found that Paganism was better. I don't like organized religions. I'm a patchwork Witch, meaning that I pick bits and pieces from all religions and throw them all together.

—KATHLEEN, FROM A TOWN IN NORTH DAKOTA

Living in a small town is much different from being in a city. In the city there tends to be lots of kinds of people all mixed together, and you're bound to find somebody else like you. In a small town it's not like that. Everybody knows everybody else, and people tend to all be very much the same. You might feel like an outsider, especially when you're still new to the Pagan lifestyle, but don't let it get to you. There are others around; you just have to find them. Take it all in stride and be honest about who you are. You're likely to be the only representative some people have of the Pagan faith, so always be honorable in your interactions with your community.

—DEANNA EBERLIN, ADDISON, NEW YORK

You [as an Emigrant] are already an outsider. Don't make it worse. Most of those who live here have always lived here. And their families have always lived here. It's already hard to fit in, so don't put flaming pentagrams in your front yard. People around here don't really advertise what religion they are, but if you start out trying to stand out, you're more likely to be ostracized.

Never underestimate who your allies will be. Some see a Baptist minister down the street and immediately think the minister will be against them. I, however, have a really good relationship with all the clergy in this town. Then one day a construction worker was in the place where I work, someone who you would think had seen it all, and saw my necklace and started yelling at me about how I was evil. So you never know.

—EVY, BOLIVAR, NEW YORK

I have found that, overall, people are very welcoming. It's all about how you present yourself. If you are kind, generous, and respectful, even people in a small town with three churches for 416 people will be good in return. Answer any questions you get as intelligently and calmly as possible. A lot of people are unfamiliar with what we believe, and I have found people are more curious than judgmental. Don't shy away, don't proclaim, just be.

My husband and I were very close with our neighbors across the street. He gave us food from his gardens; any chicken in his yard we wanted for dinner, we could ask for. They were especially interested when I started taking correspondence classes to become an herbalist. They had a gorgeous comfrey specimen that they let me split to grow my own plant. After some time they would ask questions and nod kindly and say things like "You don't say" and "You wouldn't ever believe that would work."

The husband worked construction and was often covered with bumps and bandages. One day he dropped off some potatoes for us, and he had a gaping wound on his thumb. I immediately asked him what he was going to do about it. He replied, "Nothing." After he left, I whipped up a batch of my wound-healer salve and walked it over. He was certainly skeptical as I opened this jar of jet black, smells-like-death salve. I told him to go ahead and just apply it as often as he wanted, and his body would just absorb it and his wound would heal.

I had doubts he would try it, but the very next day he came over and stuck his thumb in my face. "Look at this, it's almost closed already," he grinned. Not only did he continue to use my salve until it was gone, but he also asked me to make a big batch for future use, and their mere interest in my herbal studies turned into consultations when needed.

—WITCH OF THE WOODS, MERRIMAC, WISCONSIN

It's a farm community. There are four seasons: too hot, too cold, too wet, and too dry. I don't go outside and practice. I've noticed young people, maybe age sixteen to eighteen, go into the public parks here late at night and celebrate. I wouldn't be that brave. The park closes at dark, so they were taking a big risk. I'm more cautious.

This is definitely a Christian-based town. There's more gossip at the local diner in the morning than at the hair salon—and I'm a hairdresser!

—IRIS, GENOA, ILLINOIS

It's difficult to find other people on a non-Abrahamic path if you don't have local Pagan clergy. It's hard to meet or have a discussion group without organizing it yourself. Most people we encounter are more curious than discouraging about why we don't go to church or participate in mainstream religion.

—KIM SCHAUFENBUEL, OWATONNA, MINNESOTA

We have a significant interfaith group with representatives from different faiths and talks about Thanksgiving, Yule, and other traditions of giving thanks. We often share ideas of faith and understanding. In the last few years I've been doing a little music at the meetings, songs I've written, etc. There's always a potluck dinner afterward. The local Roman Catholics don't get involved—their local bishop told them not to attend any events with Pagans. The Greek Orthodox Catholics participate, though. This group is a great example of how all the mainline religions espouse tolerance of the other religions.

There's an annual interfaith Yule celebration at the Unitarian church that's very well attended every year. The community is invited to attend. There's often a pageant where the Holly King is ritually "killed" by the Oak King. People read poems, there's singing, the kids get involved—just so the community knows we're not sacrificing sheep.

Sometimes it just takes time and exposure.

—FERGUS, MONONA, WISCONSIN

If you are just moving into a small town, take it slow. Don't start preaching about what a big old

Witch you are. Let folks get to know you. Be a good neighbor, make sure your grass is mowed and your trash is cleaned up. Be there to help people if they need something. Volunteer for local organizations that you have something in common with, such as cleaning up local parks and wildlife areas, neighborhood watches, neighborhood gardens, etc. Give people time to get to know you for you, not because you're a Pagan.

There is great joy in living in a small town. Life has a much slower pace; it's less frantic. Small-town activities, like parades and Fourth of July picnics, are a great way to get out and know your neighbors. There is a sense of being at peace with the world and with life that I never found in large cities. Knowing who your neighbors are—having block parties and knowing your neighbors' names and their faces—and knowing that we all watch out for each other and each other's children, it's a very satisfying thing.

—JULIA, EAST STROUDSBURG, PENNSYLVANIA

We have many Pagans here, but we tend to keep things very low-key. We have learned the hard way that this town isn't ready for an Old-Time Religion Revival anytime soon. If you have children, for the love of all that is holy, ward them and spell them and hug them every day, and remind them that graduation is sooner than they think and pretty soon none of those kids who point fingers and accuse them of following Satan will remember who they are.

When you are outed as a Pagan in a small town, you will quickly find out how many of your neighbors watch way too many movies and far too much television. "Seriously, one more Charmed *quote and I swear I will hex your tires flat."*

—RAVENNA, DOWAGIAC, MICHIGAN

I really believe that many folks in small towns have descended from families that lived close to the land. Many still practice a form of folk magic. They just don't call it that. They can read the land, the weather, and understand the animals' behavior. It's kinda like they know and you know they know, and as long as no one says it out loud, we're all okay here.

—K, SEVIERVILLE, TENNESSEE

Afterthoughts

So what happens now? Is this conversation-that-looks-like-a-book over?

That, at least in part, is up to you. I hope you feel inspired to reach out to other Pagans in your area and try to at least meet at the local coffee shop even if you're not quite up to starting your own weekly or monthly meetup yet.

I was recently able to lead a discussion on "Life as a Small-Town Pagan" at a rather large Pagan gathering. The attendees had plenty to say and did not want to part from each other when the scheduled hour was over. Listening to them—and I did much more listening than talking, a rare event for me when I'm responsible for a workshop!—I was grateful that I had not experienced some of the discrimination they had;

humbled by their courage to come and share their experiences; and, ultimately, happy that I have chosen to live my life and practice my faith in a small town.

Like me, like the survey respondents in this book, the workshop attendees had much to say about the positive aspects of small-town Pagan life, particularly the closeness to, and the deeper appreciation of, the natural cycles of the year. At the end of the workshop, all the participants agreed that those of us who choose to live in small towns and call ourselves Pagans need to reach out to each other more, to communicate, to start an ongoing conversation about ourselves, our families, our lives, and our practice.

Now it's your turn to chime in.

I'm trying to keep the conversation going via the Small Town Pagans Yahoo e-mail group, at http://groups.yahoo .com/group/smalltownpagans. I hope you'll join in and contribute your thoughts and experiences. You never know when what you have to say will help someone else.

I also encourage the very bravest readers to consider attending a nearby Pagan Pride Day or gathering, and offering to facilitate your own discussion/workshop on life as a small-town Pagan. After all, if you're Pagan and you live in a small town, you have as much expertise as I do on the subject! Pagan Pride celebrations and festivals attract Pagans from all over the region, not just from the city they're nearest to. It's been my experience that there are plenty of folks in attendance who come from small towns just like yours and who really want the chance to talk about their lives.

If nothing else, I hope you now know that you're not alone. With luck, something in these pages struck a chord, and you said, "Hey, that happened to me, too!"

Recommended Reading

Bonewits, Isaac. *Neopagan Rites: A Guide to Creating Public Rituals That Work*. Woodbury, MN: Llewellyn, 2007.

Bulfinch, Thomas. *Bulfinch's Mythology*. New York: Barnes & Noble Classics, 2006. Originally published in 1881; many editions available.

Campbell, Joseph. *The Hero with a Thousand Faces*, third edition. Novato, CA: New World Library, 2008.

Eilers, Dana D. *Pagans and the Law: Understand Your Rights*. Franklin Lakes, NJ: Career Press, 2009.

Forbes, Bronwen. *Make Merry in Step and Song: A Seasonal Treasury of Music, Mummer's Plays & Celebrations in the English Folk Tradition*. Woodbury, MN: Llewellyn, 2009.

Hamilton, Edith. *Mythology*. Boston: Back Bay Books, 1998. First published in 1942.

K, Amber. *Coven Craft: Witchcraft for Three or More*. St. Paul, MN: Llewellyn, 2002.

Madden, Kristin. *Pagan Parenting: Spiritual, Magical & Emotional Development of the Child*, revised edition. Niceville, FL: Spilled Candy Publications, 2004. (Originally published by Llewellyn Publications in 2000.)

McSherry, Lisa. *Magickal Connections: Creating a Lasting and Healthy Spiritual Group*. Franklin Lakes, NJ: New Page Books, 2007.

———. *The Virtual Pagan: Exploring Wicca and Paganism through the Internet*. Boston: Weiser Books, 2002.

Resources

General Websites

The Pagan Pride Project:
http://www.paganpride.org
The Wild Hunt:
http://www.wildhunt.org/blog
Unitarian Universalist Association of Congregations:
http://www.uua.org
Internet Sacred Texts Archive:
http://www.sacred-texts.com
Myth*ing Links:
http://www.mythinglinks.org

Beliefnet:

http://www.beliefnet.com

Cauldron Living:

http://www.cauldronliving.com

The Cauldron:

http://www.ecauldron.com

Shopping Websites

AzureGreen:

http://www.azuregreen.com

CafePress:

http://www.cafepress.com

Mountain Rose Herbs:

http://www.mountainroseherbs.com

Abaxion:

http://www.abaxion.com

eBay:

http://www.ebay.com

Etsy:

http://www.etsy.com

13moons.com:

http://www.13moons.com

The Blessed Be:

http://www.theblessedbee.com

Artists' Websites

Nybor Mystical Art:

http://www.nyborart.com

Susan Seddon Boulet:

http://www.susanseddonboulet.com

Anne Marie Forrester:

http://web.mac.com/annemarieforrester

Alicia Austin:

http://www.aliciaaustin.com

Jen Delyth:

http://www.kelticdesigns.com

Mickie Mueller:

http://www.mickiemuellerart.com

Networking Sites

Witchvox:

http://www.witchvox.com

LiveJournal:

http://www.livejournal.com

Facebook:

http://www.facebook.com

Yahoo Groups:

http://www.groups.yahoo.com

Index

To Write to the Author

If you wish to contact the author or would like more information about this book, please write to the author in care of Llewellyn Worldwide Ltd. and we will forward your request. Both the author and publisher appreciate hearing from you and learning of your enjoyment of this book and how it has helped you. Llewellyn Worldwide Ltd. cannot guarantee that every letter written to the author can be answered, but all will be forwarded. Please write to:

Bronwen Forbes
% Llewellyn Worldwide
2143 Wooddale Drive
Woodbury, MN 55125-2989

Please enclose a self-addressed stamped envelope for reply, or $1.00 to cover costs. If outside the USA, enclose an international postal reply coupon.

GET MORE AT LLEWELLYN.COM

Visit us online to browse hundreds of our books and decks, plus sign up to receive our e-newsletters and exclusive online offers.

- Free tarot readings • Spell-a-Day • Moon phases
- Recipes, spells, and tips • Blogs • Encyclopedia
- Author interviews, articles, and upcoming events

GET SOCIAL WITH LLEWELLYN

Find us on
Facebook

www.Facebook.com/LlewellynBooks

Follow us on

www.Twitter.com/Llewellynbooks

GET BOOKS AT LLEWELLYN

LLEWELLYN ORDERING INFORMATION

Order online: Visit our website at www.llewellyn.com to select your books and place an order on our secure server.

Order by phone:
- Call toll free within the U.S. at 1-877-NEW-WRLD (1-877-639-9753)
- Call toll free within Canada at 1-866-NEW-WRLD (1-866-639-9753)
- We accept VISA, MasterCard, and American Express

Order by mail:
Send the full price of your order (MN residents add 6.875% sales tax) in U.S. funds, plus postage and handling to: Llewellyn Worldwide, 2143 Wooddale Drive Woodbury, MN 55125-2989

POSTAGE AND HANDLING:

STANDARD: (U.S. & Canada)
(Please allow 12 business days)
$25.00 and under, add $4.00.
$25.01 and over, FREE SHIPPING.

INTERNATIONAL ORDERS (airmail only):
$16.00 for one book, plus $3.00 for each additional book.

Visit us online for more shipping options.
Prices subject to change.

FREE CATALOG!

To order, call
1-877-
NEW-WRLD
ext. 8236
or visit our
website

MAKE
MERRY
IN STEP AND SONG

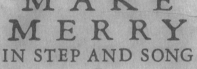

A SEASONAL TREASURY OF MUSIC,
MUMMER'S PLAYS & CELEBRATIONS
IN THE ENGLISH FOLK TRADITION

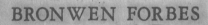

BRONWEN FORBES

Make Merry in Step and Song

A Seasonal Treasury of Music, Mummer's Plays &
Celebrations in the English Folk Tradition

BRONWEN FORBES

"See the blazing Yule before us…" This is just one of the many ancient British folk songs we all know and love. Yet other tunes and symbols that tug on our memories have similar historical roots, hearkening back to a shared Pagan past. These dances, songs, and theatrical plays in the English folk tradition are less well known to most of the modern Pagan community. Reviving these vital traditions can bring new life to Renaissance festivals, Neopagan rituals, and community events.

Introducing the lively music and homegrown entertainments of times long past, this descriptive how-to is designed for twenty-first-century joviality. The songs, dances, and plays of old are explained in their mythical, seasonal, and historical significance and outlined for easy reenactment. Simple-to-follow instructions detail six dances, including the popular Abbots Bromley Horn dance, six full scripts for dramatic performances of mummer's plays (folk plays of death and rebirth), and over thirty songs with lyrics and music. Kick up your heels, hold high your skirts, and make merry the year through.

978-0-7387-1500-1, 264 pp., 7½ x 9⅛" $19.95

NEO
PAGAN
RITES

A GUIDE TO CREATING
PUBLIC RITUALS THAT WORK

Isaac Bonewits

Neopagan Rites

A Guide to Creating Public Rituals That Work

ISAAC BONEWITS

Isaac Bonewits includes over three decades of his own ritual experience—creating, attending, and leading ceremonies as a Neopagan priest and magician—into this practical guide to effective ritual. Ideal for Earth-centered spiritual movements and other liberal religious traditions, this book clarifies how to design powerful rites for small groups as well as for large crowds.

Bonewits addresses every detail that contributes to successful public worship: the dynamics of participants, common worship patterns, the deities invoked, pre-ritual preparation, and more. Learn to choose the optimal time, location, costume, props, and altar decorations. Enhance your ceremony with music, singing, poetry, dance, and movement. There are also invaluable tips for raising and channeling energy and using centers of power to send energy. Best of all, *Neopagan Rites* will help you create and perform rituals that unify, inspire, and fulfill their intended purpose.

978-0-7387-1199-7, 240 pp., 6 x 9" $15.95

Witchcraft for Three or More

COVEN CRAFT

Amber K

Coven Craft

Witchcraft for Three or More

AMBER K

Here is the complete guidebook for anyone who desires to practice Witchcraft in a caring, challenging, well-organized spiritual support group—in other words, a coven. Whether you hope to learn more about this ancient spiritual path or are a coven member wanting more rewarding experiences in your group; whether you are looking for a coven to join or are thinking of starting one, or whether you are a Wiccan elder gathering proven techniques and fresh ideas . . . this book is for you.

Amber K shares what she has learned in her twenty years as a Wiccan priestess about beginning and maintaining healthy covens. Learn what a coven is, how it works, and how you can make your coven experience more effective, enjoyable, and rewarding. Plus, get practical hands-on guidance in the form of sample articles of incorporation, Internet resources, sample by-laws, and sample budgets. Seventeen ritual scripts are also provided.

978-1-56718-018-3, 528 pp., 7 x 10" $19.95

Pagan Spirituality

A Guide to Personal Transformation

JOYCE & RIVER HIGGINBOTHAM

In a world filled with beginner books, deeper explanations of the Pagan faith are rarely found. Picking up where their critically acclaimed first book *Paganism* left off, bestselling authors Joyce and River Higginbotham offer intermediate-level instruction with *Pagan Spirituality*.

Respected members of their communities, the Higginbothams describe, in a pleasant, encouraging tone, how to continue spiritual evolution though magick, communing, energy work, divination, and conscious creation. Learn how to use journaling, thought development, visualization, and goal-setting to develop magickal techniques and to further cultivate spiritual growth. This book serves to expand the reader's spiritual knowledge base by providing a balanced approach of well-established therapies, extensive personal experience, and question-and-answer sessions that directly involve readers in their own spiritual journey.

978-0-7387-0574-3, 288 pp., 7½ x 9⅛" $16.95

To order, call 1-877-NEW-WRLD
Prices subject to change without notice
Order at Llewellyn.com 24 hours a day, 7 days a week!